# For Fun and Profit

# For Fun and Profit
## Self-Employment Opportunities in Recreation, Sports and Travel

by Crawford Lindsey

Live Oak Publications
Boulder, Colorado

**Library of Congress Cataloging in Publication Data**

Lindsey, Crawford.
   For Fun and Profit.

   Bibliography: p.
   1. Recreation—Vocational guidance—United States.
2. Self-employed—United States. I. Title.
GV160.L56 1984    790'.023    84-47761
ISBN 0-911781-01-3

The author and publisher have attempted to ensure the accuracy of all information in this book. Errors can occur, however, and requirements for starting a business are changed from time to time and can vary from location to location. For these reasons the publisher and author disclaim responsibility for the total accuracy of this book. Professional legal and accounting advice should be sought by anyone starting a business.

ISBN: 0-911781-01-3

Library of Congress Catalog Card Number: 84-47761

Published by    Live Oak Publications
               P.O. Box 2193
               Boulder, CO 80306

# Table of Contents

*Those whose work and play are one
are fortune's favorite children.*
— Winston Churchill

# Chapter 1
# The Growing Opportunities
# in Recreation

*"We are now the most recreation-oriented society
the world has ever seen. Work is still important, of
course, but . . . we're passing out of the work ethic
mentality to a stage where people put more emphasis
on the importance of leisuretime activity."*
— Don Parkin, quoted in *Advertising Age*

There are some good reasons for taking play very
seriously today. Americans are spending more money
on recreation — including sports, travel and fitness —
than ever before, and the net result is a dramatic increase in all sorts of self-employment opportunities.

We now spend close to $250 billion annually on
recreation, and yet the growth of recreation spending
continues to break new records year after year:

- About $1 out of every $8 of consumers' personal spending now goes for recreation, *more than is spent on national defense or housing construction.*

- The growth in recreation spending appears to be virtually recession-proof.

- Spending on recreation is rising faster than overall consumer spending.

- Employment is growing more in recreation than in any other economic sector.

From wind surfing to mechanical bull riding, and from white-water rafting to racing in bathtub regattas, Americans are passionately involved in the "pursuit of happiness." A dominant characteristic of today's recreational pursuits is this wide-ranging variety which, as we shall see, gives self-employment opportunities in this field a special appeal.

## REASONS FOR THE BOOM

Several factors contribute to the explosive growth in recreation spending, and by examining them it becomes clear that recreation is likely to continue to grow in importance far into the future.

To begin with, consumers increasingly view having fun not as a luxury but as a necessity. No longer is recreation seen as something only earned through toil or reserved for the wealthy. Now it is often considered to be as important as work, and some clearly consider it to be more important.

## Health Benefits of Recreation

This changing conception of recreation results at least partly from the increased awareness of the health benefits of having fun. The current passion for fitness provides clear evidence of this awareness, with about half of all adult Americans exercising regularly now, almost twice the number that did twenty years ago.

The benefits of recreation on mental health are also better appreciated now. Many people rely on their recreational pursuits to identify who they are — a mountaineer, a fisherman, a long-distance runner. When meaningful identification is missing from career pursuits, such identification with recreation can serve an important psychological function. Used properly, recreation can also provide a healthy alternative to drug and alcohol dependency.

But beyond any specific physical or mental health benefits, play is increasingly seen as necessary for recharging our creative and emotional batteries. Executive retreats and on-site corporate fitness facilities are becoming commonplace as management recognizes the need to provide recreational opportunities which can help to prevent burnout.

Not all play is as structured as executive retreats, of course. Leslie Scott, an independent consultant for the New Games Foundation, which promotes group play based on cooperation rather than competition, provides an example of what she calls "unconscious play": "I've been in situations in school districts where I work with the staff, and people have come up to me after a play session and say, 'Did you see those two over there? They haven't talked to each other in five years.' The game I'm playing might be hug tag, where if I come to tag you, the only way you're safe is if you're hugging somebody. So they're hugging because what comes up for people in a game of tag is to do whatever it takes . . . to be safe."

**More Time for Play**

Also contributing to the boom in recreation spending is the increased leisure time available for play. The work week continues to shrink, from 38.6 hours 20 years ago to 35.3 hours now, and most people average 120 nonworking days a year. Yet, when asked whether they would prefer a pay increase or more time off, most workers continue to opt for more free time. When you combine this with the trends toward early retirement and increased life expectancy, the growth in time available for recreation becomes clear.

**Impact of Technology**

Technology is also contributing to increased recreation spending. Modern technology has made vast changes in traditional sports and made possible entirely new kinds of sports. Today's sports equipment is lighter, stronger, safer, and easier to use. Medical knowledge is now extensively applied to participatory sports, resulting in a healthier population, increased prevention and more rapid recovery from sports injuries.

## INCREASING DEMAND CREATES OUTSTANDING OPPORTUNITIES

The current burgeoning demand for recreation is not only a demand for more fun, but for more varied kinds of fun. It is this growing consumer demand for more recreational choices that translates into specific market niches — niches which are ideal opportunities for small business ventures.

If you're like most people wanting to become self-employed, you don't have a lot of capital to back you up. This being the case, you'll be far better off not trying to compete directly with the well-financed corporations which dominate many of the largest recreation markets.

The real opportunities for you are in the smaller, more highly specialized markets which are constantly springing up as recreation consumers express more varied interests and demand more choices. These specialized markets are usually too small to attract much interest from large corporations, but they can be extremely rewarding for anyone with the interest and determination to seek them out.

Again and again throughout this book we refer to "targeting your market." If you're an individual using a bare-bones budget to build your business you simply can't afford to try to be all things to all people. You must tightly focus your efforts on whatever population group, or customer market, you've selected to offer your product or service to. Don't try to beat the corporate giants at their own game — it's futile and unnecessary when there are so many other opportunities just waiting to be tapped.

## SELF-EMPLOYMENT: A REALISTIC GOAL

As the dramatic increase in recreation spending has taken place, another trend, the re-emergence of self-employment, has also occurred. For 50 years, until the beginning of the 1970s, self-employment was on the decline as big business consolidated its power. With the coming of the 1970s the pendulum began swinging back the other way, and by the end of the decade self-employment had increased an impressive 29 percent. The economies of scale and the advantages of centralization which large corporations had previously enjoyed have now given way to the strengths inherent in small businesses: flexibility, speed, and the ability to keep costs carefully under control.

Other factors also contributed to the surge in

self-employment. At about this time the baby boom generation began to come of age, and there were simply not enough jobs to go around for the huge numbers of well-educated young people entering the workforce.

It was not only the shear size of the baby boom generation that created problems, however. This generation was unusually idealistic, and tended to place much more emphasis on job satisfaction over job pay. The independence possible through self-employment had great appeal to the baby boomers, an appeal often made irresistible by the scarcity of interesting salaried jobs.

It was also about this time that our national economy began to shift from a manufacturing orientation to a service orientation. Manufacturing requires large capital investments and takes full advantage of the purchasing power of large corporations. Services, on the other hand, require the least capital of any type of business and are the easiest businesses to start. Furthermore, small *can* be beautiful with service businesses, where the personal touch of a dedicated owner can lead to loyal customers and word-of-mouth advertising.

One final factor contributing to the increase in self-employment concerns the growing consumer demand for variety and choice in the marketplace. Until the 1970s, consumers were easily satisfied. There was no need for 15 different types of bread, because white sandwich bread seemed to be all that anyone wanted. General interest magazines such as *Life* and *Post* enjoyed huge circulations, and few suspected they would give way to hundreds of special interest publications covering every conceivable subject.

Why did consumers begin to demand more variety and choice? It didn't really occur until an entire generation had grown up without having experienced anything other than prosperity. For those who experienced the depression, *any* bread on the table is easily appreciated. But those born after the depression grew up with the idea that it is possible to express your identity and uniqueness through the products and services you buy.

## ADVANTAGES OF SELF-EMPLOYMENT

The best way to appreciate the advantages of self-employment is to talk to those already succeeding in their chosen ventures. Talking to people who are self-employed in recreation can be a delight. The enthusiasm with which they talk reflects their commitment to and the high-energy nature of their sports/fitness/recreation activity. For these people, work is far more than a job; it is also their fulfillment. This aspect clearly comes through in the following comments, which are typical of remarks made by many of those interviewed for this book.

Eric Bader, kayak outfitter, manufacturer, and teacher: "I've been kayaking for a long time. I love the sport, I love teaching it. I worked with clubs, I made gear, and as a matter of fact, I did light manufacturing to support my own boating for the weekends. . . . I worked for a couple of other companies and decided I'd rather work for myself. I could do a better job, and it was a field that I was qualified in, so I decided to go into business.

"I definitely do it for the love of the sport; otherwise, I would have definitely gotten out of it by now and just worked for someone else nine to five for a paycheck every week or two weeks. . . . You have to do it because you love it."

Miriam Gingras, corporate fitness consultant: "I wanted to start a business that was a real challenge to me and something that I really believed in."

Gary Neptune, mountaineering shop owner: "I was a climber first, and then when I was in grad school I began to realize that I really wasn't that interested in what I was doing and didn't especially want to make a career out of it, although I certainly could have. . . . Climbing, for me, must have been more of a passion . . . but obviously I wanted to do it, and it seemed like this was one way to make it work.

". . . I quit [school] almost as a commitment. . . . My parents would say, 'you ought to finish that up so you'll have something to fall back on' . . . and in a sense, that is exactly what I didn't want."

Robert Hackworth, events management consultant: "I just kind of got fed up with working in bureaucratic situations and decided I wanted to work for myself. So, the first thing that I do is hang out a shingle that says, 'For hire, Robert Hackworth, consultant.'

"My interest in sports and recreation goes back to the fact that I was involved in the sport of running, both as trying to be an entrepreneur and also trying to be an athlete and competing on a national-class basis. So it was real important that I could tie those two together.

"In fact, one of the real motivating factors toward becoming self-employed was to have the flexibility and the freedom to continue to train, to travel, to compete, and all those things you want to do."

Barbara Wakshul, holistic health counselor: "I'm really interested in my work being exciting and interesting and varied, and if I'm going to spend a fair amount of time at it, it's got to support me on more than just the financial level. I have found in the last several years that work can do that, and you just have to be clear about what you want and why you want it."

The common theme in these comments is that self-employment provides benefits above and beyond financial compensation. These benefits include self-expression through your work, self-reliance, independence, integration of your work with your lifestyle, the satisfaction of meeting challenges head-on and seeing the results of your own hard work. Pride of ownership is another frequently mentioned benefit, and the ability to provide employment opportunities to family members or friends can also be important.

## THE QUESTION OF CREDENTIALS

Generally speaking, the people interviewed for this book are not terribly concerned about acquiring a degree in recreation, a master's in business administration, or other credentials. The business ventures described are often logical extensions of the individual's background and interests. A commitment to self-expression and the full use of personal skills and talents seem to serve many of these people better than any credentials they might acquire, and in many cases a reliance on inner logic and resourcefulness effectively replaces reliance on standard business practices.

This is not to imply that the people interviewed, and others self-employed in recreation, are not serious about their work. These are people who have invested in themselves, and most have clearly made long-term commitments to their chosen work.

There is a difference in priorities between these new-age entrepreneurs and conventional, established business people, however. The largest possible return on investment is not necessarily the source of motivation for those interviewed, and growth at all costs is rarely seen as a goal. More often, it is personal fulfillment and the integration of a satisfying worklife with all other aspects of their lives that these people are seeking.

But how do you convince other people that you are qualified if you don't have the "proper credentials"? Robert Hackworth, the events management consultant, just shrugs off the question, saying "Well, if I can't go that route, I'll have to take another route. The other route is to start my own projects. . . . I come to myself and say, 'you're hired.' "

## KEYS TO SUCCESS

There is no question that the surge in recreation spending is creating unprecedented opportunities. Likewise, conditions are becoming increasingly favorable for self-employment.

In spite of these well-established trends, it would be foolhardy to rush into self-employment in recreation (or any other field) without a great deal of thought, planning, and care. There is risk involved in any small business venture, and it is important to do everything possible to minimize this risk while maximizing your chances of success.

There are a variety of books devoted to small business start-ups (see appendix), and you should read as many of them as practical. In general terms, taking the following steps will vastly improve your chances of success.

• Try to find a way to fully use your experience and interests. Ask yourself what competitive advantages you can put to use. Your enthusiasm for your business can have a powerful influence on your success.

• Research your market. The more you know about your customers the better you'll be able to serve them. Market research can be conducted simply and inexpensively, and excellent books are available to guide you.

• Keep your overhead low. Always try the least expensive forms of promotion first — even if they don't work, you'll learn valuable lessons from them. If you can work out of your home in the beginning, do so.

• Talk to people already in business. You'll probably find them extremely informative unless you will be in direct competition with them. In that case, go to another city to find people who won't have to worry about a distant competitor.

• Try to avoid hiring employees. Because of the enormous amounts of paperwork they require and the tax and insurance expenses involved, you'll probably be better off using contract labor initially.

• Don't grow too big too fast. Carefully controlled growth allows you to match cash flow to expenses and prevent becoming dangerously overextended.

• Remember to take a break occasionally. Even people intensely involved with recreation can experience burnout. A period spent away from your business can provide fresh motivation and valuable new insights.

# Chapter 2
# Opportunities in Physical Fitness

When jogging, aerobics and health food began sweeping the country in the 1970s, many regarded concern with fitness to be just another fad, destined to go the way of the Hula Hoop.

Today fitness is often regarded as a national obsession, but no longer is it considered a fad. It is much too well-established and too multidimensional to be a fad, and few if any fads have become as much a part of everyday American life and transformed the nation's character as much as the current passion for fitness, youthfulness, and physical beauty.

Studies of societal attitudes and trends consistently indicate that concerns with fitness are growing in importance. Slowly but steadily the contagious nature of fitness has spread to more and more segments of American society. Many people over 65 are becoming involved in fitness programs for the first time in their lives, and fitness programs for infants are gradually becoming popular. There are programs for the handicapped, for the seriously overweight, and for recuperating heart attack patients, too.

About half of all adult Americans, in fact, now engage in some sort of fitness activity — a dramatic increase from 24 percent in 1960. Even President Reagan has gotten into the act, recently installing a Universal-type weight machine in the family quarters of the White House.

At least partly as a result of this passion for fitness, heart disease, the nation's number one health problem, has decreased some 20 percent since 1967. Strokes are down by one-third, while there has been an increase in life expectancy to a record 73 years.

Another result, more relevant to the theme of this book, is that exploding demand has created enormous sales increases for all types of fitness-related products and services, and entirely new types of fitness markets (and opportunities) have sprung up. Consider the following:

• Americans now spend $5 billion annually on health clubs and fitness centers.

• The market for sport shoes alone has reached $1 billion.

• $240 million annually goes for barbells and aerobic dance programs.

• Today the age of the average owner of an exercise bicycle is 45 — 10 years younger than in 1978. The percentage of U.S. families owning exercise bikes is now over 7 percent, compared with 1 percent just a few years ago.

With fitness-related markets expanding so rapidly, opportunities for self-employment are growing too. The question for most people is "How do I get started?" Usually you find a need which is not being met, and come up with a plan to fill the need.

## IT ALL BEGINS WITH AN IDEA

In defense of her profession, Jody Stock states "There is a lot more to being an aerobics teacher than being able to jump up and down and smile." And, as Jody also found out, owning and managing an aerobics fitness center requires more than simply finding a space and hanging a sign on the front door.

That sign — Jody's Sweat Shop — signifies that what once was just an idea is now a thriving business, however, and Jody, who once was "only" a mom, is now a successful business owner. For her, learning the ins and outs of effective business management was the most difficult hurdle: "just learning to deal with personnel, how to pick managers, how to tell them what you want, and how to make sure that they are doing what you want."

When Jody started Jody's Sweat Shop, aerobics

was still an activity dependent upon support from larger facilities. The only aerobics classes generally available were offered as part of a large organization's menu of activities. Jody gave aerobics a life of its own. "Most people thought I was crazy," she admits, "but I knew it would work." Her conviction was partly based on her perception that there was a market of "imprisoned women" that nobody had yet tapped: "When you really need to go [exercise] is when your children are real small, and here in town nobody would babysit kids under three, and that's when you need to get out." Jody believed that women with small children were somewhat imprisoned in their homes because of the lack of activities available that offered child care. "I was a woman who had gone through this and knew what they liked and knew they needed a babysitter, and they needed a nice babysitting room where they could leave their kids and not feel guilty."

This was no facile observation. In a day and age when we are told that Mom has been liberated from the household, Jody saw that this was just not always true. She provided a setup where mothers with young children could escape for an hour or two, and the women responded in force. Jody had cornered her market.

Judy Shepard Misset, the founder of the international franchise organization Jazzercise, also noticed a market niche that was not being served. According to Tracy Van de Boogaard, a Jazzercize franchise owner, Judy was teaching dance classes to children when she first realized that a large void existed. "There were calisthenic type programs and structured technical dance classes, and those were your choices for both women and men. There wasn't anything in between to combine the two where you've got the aerobic, cardiovascular, heart and lung workout along with the feel of dance." Judy was convinced the gap represented a need and an opportunity, and she proceeded to develop programs combining the "stretching, flexability, coordination, posture, balance and stamina [of dance] with the . . . entire aerobic, cardiovascular segment." She began teaching her program to the mothers of her young students, and the rest is history — stepped out by 2,500 independent franchised instructors and their 300,000 students.

## PLANNING AND FINANCING YOUR BUSINESS

A dream and a concept is rarely enough to launch a business, of course. For Jody the next step involved convincing the landlord "that I wasn't a flake. He thought I would last about two months — and then [I had to] convince the banker that it wasn't just a hair-brained idea." She convinced both, and with a $20,000 loan and one month of lead time she opened the area's first drop-in aerobics fitness center.

What did it take to get started? Jody used "every cent" of the $20,000 loan. Big ticket items included:

- Rent (two months up front)
- Stereo equipment
- Printing (for promotional flyers) "I spent thousands on that."
- Advertising — "It's easy to drop a couple of thousand on a couple of weeks of advertising."

These expenses, coupled with the monetary demands of surviving the first months of being open, led Jody to offer some very simple advice to people thinking of opening similar businesses: "If you haven't got enough money to tide you over for six months or a year, you shouldn't open the business." This is wholeheartedly endorsed by Donna Farentinos, another aerobics studio owner who recommends planning on a year of scraping to get by. "You have to plan ahead for how you are going to eat."

Donna and her husband Bob also own a gym, but theirs is different from Jody's Sweat Shop in that it specializes in resistance weight training. The lead time required for researching and arranging the financing for an operation like theirs will be longer than the two months Jody needed. Bob spent a year and a half researching and selecting equipment for their gym, and the time was well spent: "It was a very calculated risk. . . . I knew what I was getting into, and it worked out pretty close to what I had anticipated." It took eighteen months to break even, but Bob had anticipated that amount of time so it was built into the financial plans for the business. Of course there is nothing magical about the eighteen months figure. It was simply a planned amount of time derived from the financing structure (composed of cash, equity, and borrowed funds) and from the amount of business projected from his market research.

**Venture Capitalists**

Mike Keel, the owner of an exercise studio that caters to the low and middle ranges of the fitness spectrum, had a slightly different experience. In order to finance his business he had to approach venture capitalists. Why? "We are not bankable. The reason we are not bankable is that we have no inventory, we have no assets, we have nothing the bank . . . can take if we fail. So, the bank doesn't want to involve itself with a service operation of our type."

Because Mike chose prime rental space in the middle of town and extensive remodeling was required, he needed a total of $60,000 to open: $10,000 for rent, $40,000 for remodeling, and $10,000 for salaries and advertising. This is quite a contrast to the $20,000 Jody spent opening her aerobics center.

Despite the large sums involved, Mike has a shorter time frame for breaking even than either Jody or Bob: "I planned a ninety day buildup to break-even, so I came in ready to lose money for three months. I want to break even in my peak hours at the end of thirty days. Next month I want to double the

peak hours.'' This is an important calculation because exercise studios of all types are often supported
by their peak-hour business. The off hours may pay
for all variable expenses and contribute some to the
fixed costs, and are therefore worthwhile, but it is the
peak-hour business that provides the ''bread and but-
ter'' for the business. This is especially true for operations that depend on drop-in customers — who pay
an hourly fee — as opposed to businesses that primarily depend on long-term memberships and a dues-
paying clientel.

### Problems in Investor/Banker/Manager Relations

Most large, multi-purpose exercise clubs are
owned by groups of individuals with investment
money. Day-to-day operations in such clubs are di-
rected by professional managers. Mike Keel, who has
worked in a variety of capacities for a number of
clubs, sees this as the reason that ''there's so much
lack of focus in the operations . . . they can't get the
profits the owners want.'' It becomes a three-ring cir-
cus, in Mike's opinion. The manager does the work,
makes the decisions, and then becomes self-serving or
loses interest. Unfortunately, this is a common criti-
cism of many of the big athletic clubs. Mike sees this
as a conflict between the owner's desire to pay the
huge debt service and make an immediate profit, and
the operator's desire to nurture the club through its
infancy into a strong, mature business. ''What I see in
the big clubs . . . goes back to the old capitalist greed

feeling that we've got to make money *now*. A big facility takes a lot of money to build. . . . After it is paid for, though, it can make a hellacious amount of profit. Owners don't see that. Owners see that they've got to be able to pay their debt service *and* make money within the first couple of years." It is this perceived conflict of interest that Mike hopes to avoid by someday opening a club by himself with only a funding relationship with a bank (as opposed to an equity partner relationship). To do this, Mike sees using the next few years to build a relationship with a bank in order to anchor his "dream club" in reality.

**Franchising and "Shoestring" Operations**

At the other end of the financing spectrum it is possible to buy a franchise, sometimes for very little money. Tracy Van de Boogaard estimates that buying into a Jazzercise franchise, for example, costs no more than $2,000-3,000, which includes the franchise fee, video player, record player, records, leotards, and video programs supplied by Jazzercise. You buy a name, organization, and reputation, and you just have to find a space to hold your classes. In some areas this is also supplied by Jazzercise (for an additional fee).

At the lowest end of the financial investment ladder, it is also possible to make a living by teaching fitness activities with no up front money whatsoever. This usually involves teaching for various clubs and recreation centers as an independent contractor. They supply the space, you supply the services, and, as we shall see, in some situations this type of arrangement can be surprisingly lucrative.

## TYPICAL START-UP PROBLEMS

Since her bare bones beginnings four years ago, Jody Stock has opened three new aerobic fitness centers, and has become the model that others copy and the standard against which others are judged. Jody is well aware that others have copied her program, taking all of her forms, studying her routines and her administrative setup. She watches the spies and thieves with a curious sort of envy, thinking to herself, "Oh you lucky dog . . . if I only had somebody to copy like that." Being the originator of the concept in her area, she didn't have anyone to copy from, and she had to realize her position of being respected and emulated by learning many lessons along the way.

What was her biggest hurdle? "Just being naive," she says matter-of-factly. She didn't know anything about hiring teachers or putting a schedule together, and as a result she wasted a lot of money: "I really learned the hard way, by trial and error."

Fortunately Jody opened her business during the slow summer months, and she was able to learn some valuable lessons without losing too much money or too many customers. One of these lessons involved the discovery that running a business by the "honor system" does not always work. Mothers were supposed to put fifty cents in the till for babysitting services while they worked out, for example. It didn't take a financial wizard to see that twenty-five "screaming kids" and two dollars in the till didn't balance out. Some customers would do things like sign up and pay for two or three days a week and then show up to exercise for all seven, and a favorite of the college kids was to arrive at Jody's in herds of ten or fifteen and storm in the door, dispersing throughout the class before the hapless front desk person could corral more than three or four paying customers.

These were three simple problems with simple solutions: 1) requiring payment before customers could leave their children for babysitting, 2) implementing a punch card system to keep track of customers' payments, and 3) using gates to channel customers individually to the cashier. "We had to get a lot stricter," says Jody of these experiences. "You have to have set rules and stick by them. . . . Once the customers understood [the rules], all of our problems ceased."

This might all seem obvious but it is all easily overlooked when you are concerned with other things such as hiring teachers or developing exercise routines. When the time to deal with these matters does arrive, however, you may discover that setting up rules is not all that you must do. You might also have to take a look at yourself and separate out the nice guy who is everyone's best buddy from the business person that keeps the operation afloat. Jody had to do just this: "I had to change my whole outlook on things. I wasn't a businesswoman, and I didn't know how to say things to people. . . . We had to get stricter. I wanted to say, 'Hey folks, I have a lot of bills to pay; this is not free.' It was really intimidating to me to say, 'I'm sorry, have you paid?' I felt as if I should apologize to someone."

## TARGETING YOUR MARKET

A great many start-up problems can be anticipated and avoided by doing the proper research before opening up shop. Market research will allow you to identify a specific segment of the population that you want to direct your services to. This includes identifying a need, determining who needs it, and putting together a service that best meets the need. You may discover needs that people don't realize they have. If you can identify services that people are not aware of needing but which are of definite benefit, you can successfully market them to a target population. It is in this way that Jody Stock saw that mothers didn't have an opportunity to exercise, and that Judy Shepard Misset realized that combining dance and aerobics together would appeal to an untouched market of people who previously thought that exercise was boring, repetitive and competitive.

Identifying needs that people are not aware of is not the same thing as projecting nonexistent needs upon the market you are targeting. Viisha Sedlack, the owner of a business called Interfit, notes that "there is a tremendous amount of opportunity for the entrepreneur in health, recreation and fitness; however, there has got to be a lot of common sense. There has to be a recognition of what people really need, not what you want — what 'I' the business person feels should be forced on the market. It never works in any business."

## Sex, Population Density, and Other Factors

A variety of factors should be considered in targeting your market. One such factor is sex. It is true that some fitness activities appeal equally to either sex, in which case sex is not an important factor, but in other fitness activities it could be disastrous to disregard its importance. In the field of aerobics, for example, women are currently the mainstay of business. The reasons for this are numerous, but many men see aerobics classes as being primarily for women and, as Jody Stock put it, "you can't convince men that no one is talking about them." Also, many men feel uncomfortable with the movements in aerobics because they are too "dancy."

It is worth noting, however, that in this example the barriers to participation by both sexes are more perceptual than real, and times do change. There may well be a broadening in the appeal of aerobics, especially considering the influence of popular dance movies that make "sports" heroes out of male dancers.

Sex is just one factor to consider in targeting the market for the fitness activity you're interested in promoting, and there are many others. The location, population density, and affluence of your market can be equally critical. Mike Keel, for example, is aiming his marketing efforts at a six-block area densely populated with business people. Supporting your business from such a small area may be hard for you to imagine, but Mike has a prime downtown location with a high concentration of affluent consumers. His target market is often pressed for time and places a high premium on accessibility, and Mike should do quite well.

Donna Farentinos, on the other hand, is targeting the entire southern half of town in her marketing efforts. This is a residential area with a much more highly dispersed clientel than Mike's. What type of people go to an aerobics center in a residential area? Housewives, after hours business people, mothers with young children and any combination thereof. There is some overlap in the market between Donna's and Mike's studios, but Donna does not see herself competing with Mike's business downtown because of the difference in their clientel.

### Coping With Different Fitness Levels

Market research should not be limited to determining demographic information (sex, age, location) about your target population. Equally important is determining the level of fitness of your clientel and the factors that motivate them to improve their fitness level, whatever it may be.

When aerobics studios first started opening up, these factors were rarely taken into account. In the early days a hundred or so people of widely differing abilities would be crowded together into a room with an instructor who tried to get them all to jump and run around together for an hour. The poor, slumped-over, dripping wet people in the back row were told not to feel self-conscious and discouraged because everybody else in the room was in the same (poor) shape at one time. Naturally a great deal of frustration resulted.

Mike Keel was one of those who recognized the disparity in abilities and felt that certain populations were not being adequately served: "What I was seeing," said Mike, "is something that is not uncommon to the fitness market anywhere, and that is that most of the programs concentrate on a 10 to 15 percent spectrum of the market." The "cream" of the market Mike refers to, of course, is the population which is highly educated and motivated about their fitness needs. These individuals already know what their fitness options are and don't have to be persuaded or sold. A much larger market exists in the rest of the population, however, and it is this group of more average fitness consumers that Mike has chosen to direct his attentions to.

Diedre Szarabajka is an independent aerobics teacher who deliberately concentrates on the 10 to 15 percent of educated and motivated fitness consumers.

She fully admits that she "doesn't appeal to the masses" because she is "too hard." She wouldn't have it any other way, however, because she gets the most enjoyment out of serving this particular type of person. And serve them she does: some of her classes have as many as two hundred people.

## Motivational Factors

As you choose the market segment you want your fitness business to appeal to you will need to consider the factors that motivate people to seek out exercise programs. It's important to appreciate the motivating factors of your particular market, whatever it might be, and to see these factors as a part of your customers' overall lifestyle.

Diedre offered this account of what motivates people to join exercise programs: "It's fun, there's a social setting, . . . a competitive edge to it. . . . People see that consistency brings results." The key statement here is that exercise can be *fun!* Many, many people subscribe to the idea of "no pain, no gain," and the possibility of having fun while exercising has often been overlooked. To really be successful marketing and promoting fitness you should personally believe exercise can be fun and be able to communicate that belief to your customers. Enthusiasm can be a powerful influence on your success.

Mike Keel has tried to identify and target people's motives. He feels that fitness classes need a new philosophy and approach that escapes the narrow sports and athletic conditioning mentality. Mike believes that "Most of the people who get involved in fitness facilities don't know how to be fit. They want to be fit, but they only want to be fit enough that they can play [sports] the way they want to and not have it penalize them. And that's really the bottom line." In other words, they don't want to hurt the rest of the week as a penalty for having a little bit of weekend fun.

Donna Farentinos admits to starting out with an illusion about people's motives. Her beginning assumption was that "people were looking for true fitness. . . . I thought they really wanted to get in here and sweat and work and just go for it like mad. I'm learning now that a lot of it is really a fad, and they just want to be able to say that they worked out."

## PACKAGING: EXPERTISE VS. HARDWARE

If targeting your market is one side of the equation for launching a successful fitness business, packaging the service you're offering is the other side. Bob Farentinos emphasizes expertise in promoting his gym. Although the gym has "state-of-the-art" equipment, it is Bob's knowledge (he is a nationally ranked cross-country skier for his age group and has a Ph.D. degree in biology) that makes working out there a unique experience. The Farentinos gym looks like any other room containing exercise equipment, but Bob has worked hard at providing a multi-dimensional exercise experience. "The hardware is used for many different kinds of applications. It is not just weight lifting or body building. . . . It is training in athletics." The message is that the service offered is more than use of the gym's hardware, and that use transcends appearance. Bob's strategy is to "de-emphasize the hardware and physical facility, even though we have the state of the art in terms of resistance training . . . we emphasize the application, the experience, and the knowledge of the exercise needs of people with different goals. That sets us apart. That is why in just two years we have had to expand the gym."

Bob has gone to a great deal of trouble to piece together a variety of exercise machines from different manufacturers based on his estimation of which are best for achieving specific results. Why does he go to such lengths when he can simply purchase a self-contained line of equipment from one manufacturer? That would really be nothing but "taking someone else's product and marketing it." In Bob's opinion, it is "not a valid approach" to purchase the equipment, line people up and send them through the manufacturer's routines by the numbers — 1, 2, 3, 4. Bob strongly feels that it makes no sense for people with different abilities training for different sports to all do the same routines. Breaking out of this production-line method of physical fitness requires expertise and knowledge, however.

Tracy Van de Boogaard is also able to offer expertise to her clients. She describes her Jazzercise program in these terms: "It's very physiologically sound from beginning to end. In class, we start with a warm-up routine, nice slow stretching to get everything going. We go into a jazz isolation routine, which is taken basically from jazz technique isolating one part of the body . . . and then we start going into the cardiovascular section where we start off lightly and we build and go to a peak area, and we go down again. We end with a nice, slow, stretchy, up routine."

Bob's and Tracy's programs are both physiologically sound, but in different ways. Whereas Bob is individualizing people's programs for specific sports or personal needs, Tracy is offering a physiologically sound program for people who just want to gain a general level of fitness. This is not to say that Tracy can't individualize somewhat in her program, however. To do so she uses albums and 45s instead of tapes so she can fit the music to the mood of the class, and people can also make requests. There are thirteen different routines in a class segment with different types of music from classical to pop, and all routines have a variety of movements so everyone can find something to their liking.

Another aspect of packaging relates to the personal touch the owner is able to provide, and this is one of the advantages that allow small businesses to compete with much larger, better financed operations. Large fitness clubs almost always have absentee owners. Bob Farentinos said "I think that is the reason for the demise of a lot of clubs — that the owners aren't there, and it gets away from them. Nobody is going to sell the place the way you sell it, not even your best employee. [Absentee ownership] is a big mistake on a small business level like this. That's one of the shortcomings of the bigger clubs. They are not owned by the people who are doing the things that the club represents." He summed up by saying "I feel that my presence, since my name is out on the sign, is very important here."

Sometimes "being present" can be taxing for the owner, of course. Jody Stock describes the realities of being an aerobics studio owner like this: "It's twenty four hours. . . . It does look so easy, but people just don't know what it's like to have someone call you at six in the morning or ten at night saying, 'I'm locked out, the electricity went off, the record player won't work, the air conditioner broke, the vacuum cleaner blew up . . . the babysitter is sick . . . your teacher just had a car wreck. Can you come down here and substitute?' My life is like that."

## HIRING, TRAINING AND SUPERVISING INSTRUCTORS

Hiring and training your teachers is on a level of importance with targeting your market and packaging your services, because your teachers represent your business to your customers and the community at large. Some aerobics/fitness instructors develop followings of such loyalty that they take on the dimensions of some kind of exercise guru. A proper training program can be crucial to developing this kind of talent.

Tracy Van de Boogaard does the screening and interviewing for Jazzercise in her region. She observes that "not everyone who wants to become an instructor is meant to become an instructor." She uses a variety of criteria to judge a person's teaching ability. First she watches them lead a class with an eye toward movement: "Can they move, are their moves sharp and clean and easy to follow? Do they have a lot of energy?"

Other qualities are assessed by Tracy in an interview:

• Are they easy to talk to?
• Do they maintain eye contact?
• What kind of appearance do they have?
• How is their public speaking?
• What is their background? Does it include business experience?
• Have they dealt with large groups of people before?
• Do they have CPR training?
• Do they have a physiology background?

If these check out, the aspiring instructor must attend two weekend training sessions.

The training to become a Jazzercise instructor may be a little more rigorous than most because it also involves acquiring an independent franchise.

However, Jody Stock also has an extensive training program for her "Jody's Sweat Shop" instructors.

Jody encountered unexpected but bearable problems in developing her training program. One of the biggest problems was the prevalence of other studios preying on her free and ready-made pool of trained instructors. "Other fitness places like to come hire my teachers," Jody said half with pride and half defensively. In order to protect herself she now requires her teachers to sign a contract which stipulates that they will only work for Jody, and if they quit, they cannot work for anyone else for a full year within a twenty mile radius of any of Jody's shops.

"I'm willing to spend a lot of time with them and teach them to be good instructors, but I have to know they are committed to me too. I couldn't put a lot into a person knowing he is going to go down the block and work for them in two weeks."

Diedre Szarabajka, an independent instructor, disagrees with the use of a contract to enforce loyalty. She imagines a judge ruling on an instructor's breach of contract suit by saying to the shop owner, "It's true, you put your time and effort into this guy, but that is the risk every employer takes. . . . It's up to you to keep the incentive there." Contracts like this do indicate a certain stability of the employee's intentions, although they may not be absolutely binding.

## LEGAL PRECAUTIONS

Teacher contracts are one of the legal precautions you should consider taking in opening a fitness business. Other precautions include the following:

- Liability insurance
- Liability release waivers for your customers to sign
- Signs that are placed in conspicuous locations announcing that the fitness center is not responsible for injury or loss of personal property

Even with these precautions, however, you can still be sued. The most common type of suit is for negligence, and your best defense is to make very, very sure that all of your instructors know what they are talking about. This is no guarantee, but it is the best preventive measure available.

It is worth noting here that although there are currently no certification requirements for aerobics instructors, there may well be in the near future.

## ADVERTISING

Having determined and targeted your market and developed and packaged your service, you must now make people aware that your service exists. Advertising is expensive, and most of the fitness entrepreneurs interviewed in this book have relied on less expensive approaches whenever possible. Advertising may be unavoidable at certain times of the year in order to announce special events or changes in your programs, however, and it can be extremely important when your business is just starting up. You have to let it be known that you exist before word of mouth (the preferred type of advertising) takes over.

Why is this important? As Donna Farentinos puts it, "Word of mouth is absolutely the best advertising. . . . As long as you offer people what they want, a good atmosphere and some knowledge to back you up, there's no reason why you can't do well."

Bob, Donna's husband, advertises his gym another way — by sponsoring elite athletes and sporting events. Top-notch athletes are allowed to work out free because Bob feels there's no better exposure than having world-class athletes say they work out at your gym. Farentinos Gym also sponsors bike racing teams, a running race, and special events (such as Viisha Sedlack's 900-mile cross-country run). Because these approaches are good at targeting the type of market Bob is trying to reach, they can be extremely cost effective. "Viisha is a case in point. She's worth thousands of dollars in newspaper ads. All she has to do is say that she trains here."

## PUBLICITY

Another advantage of sponsorship is the publicity it generates. Viisha, for example, is running to get publicity for Interfit, her own fitness business. Viisha explains: "This isn't just some crazy runner going off into the horizon. This is business. If you are going to make a business go, people have to know about it, and I want people to know about me. . . . I'm Interfit's product."

**Networking**

Mike Keel has another method of promotion in mind — networking. The beauty of networking is that it helps everyone and is noncompetitive. Mike is planning to publish what he calls a "generic fitness newsletter," for example, which all fitness organizations in town can chip in to print and distribute. This would not involve "hype" but rather information about services and activities and fitness in general. Also, as Mike sees it, he and his counterparts in the fitness field can come together to do cooperative ventures such as fitness fairs and races.

Although this type of networking makes the public aware of your competitors, it also makes them aware of how you differ from your competitors. Informing the public that approaches to fitness can be different allows them to more intelligently choose a program which meets their needs.

This is taken one step further by Mike, who believes that "any way I can promote health and fitness, I can't lose." Put differently, every convert to fitness is a potential customer. "I am already developing a cooperative network between the different fitness operators in town and the people who are involved with promoting fitness and health: the holistic chiropractors . . . the massage therapists, the nutritionists, the Wellness Center at the university, the performance lab . . . . I'm already orchestrating a lot of communication between those people. . . . I plan on really solidifying that and using that kind of educational tool to make our impact on the market, to be associated with an intelligent approach to fitness and health."

Even if advertising were not so expensive, Mike would be unlikely to abandon his low-key approach to promotion. "I don't want to be doing it with 'two for ones' all the time. I don't want to be cheapening the product and using gimmicks all the time to make sales."

## INCOME POTENTIAL

How much money can you expect to make in a fitness business? Most of the people interviewed were understandably reluctant to discuss explicit income figures. Nevertheless, some success speaks for itself. Jody Stock, for example, would be unlikely to expand into four aerobics centers unless she was making money somewhere along the way. Of course, as Jody says, "It depends on what you are in it for, and how you go about it. There are teachers who are on their own, who just rent facilities, [who] probably make more money than I do because they never put more money back into it. . . . They are in it for the short haul. . . . They literally have no expenses.''

Diedre Szarabajka is a teacher with few expenses. She teaches aerobics on contract with a university recreation center and makes approximately $24,000 a year for her part-time work. Diedre's arrangement is quite good. Students and others pay for a ten-week session which includes a total of thirty hours of classes. From these gross receipts the recreation center takes 15 percent and Diedre keeps 85 percent. Depending on the day, Diedre averages seventy to 150 people per class and sometimes can make $50-$70 an hour. On average she works twenty to twenty-five hours a week, and this includes setting up, travel, preparing her routines, making her tapes, and lingering in the shower. And what is perhaps best about this arrangement besides the low overhead is that she doesn't have ''any hassles, any worries. . . . I go in and do my own thing.''

Diedre has a friend who has an even better arrangement. She rents a large space for $45 an hour and teaches 100-200 people per class at $2 per person. She has two classes in a row. That means she can net up to $710 for two hours of work. And her ''work'' is a little different from Diedre's. Instead of exercising herself, she simply talks her way through the class!

Lori Greenstein is a yoga and belly dance instructor who contracts to teach with the same university as Diedre. She has to limit her yoga classes to twenty people in order for them to be truly effective, so her income is limited also.

The following is Lori's teaching arrangement:

- three beginning yoga classes meeting once a week for six weeks at $20 per person.
- three continuing yoga classes meeting once a week for six weeks at $20 per person.
- one belly dance class meeting once a week for six weeks at $20 per person.

This works out to 140 people × $20 = $2,800. Subtracting 15 percent for the recreation center, equals $2,380 for a six-week period, working only seven hours a week. This amounts to $56.66 per hour, which is the maximum amount possible under the above arrangement. Because some classes are not full and the fee varies between $15 and $20 per session (depending on whether students are members of the recreation center), Lori only made $1,800 in the last six-week session, or $42.85 per hour.

Tracy Van de Boogaard offers the following example of how much a person might make with a Jazzercise franchise. Suppose you make $1,000 in a month teaching Jazzercise. Your expenses would consist of the following:

- Rent: usually about 20 percent of gross or $20 per hour
- Jazzercise commission: you pay Jazzercise 30 percent of the above net, which pays for use of the name, choreography, handouts, national advertising, newsletters, and operational costs of the national staff
- Liability coverage of $50 per year

- Leotards and tights
- Printing of your own handouts
- Office supplies
- Bookkeeping
- Records and video tapes
- Stereo player and video player
- Phone
- Taxes

And what do you take home after expenses are subtracted from your gross receipts? Tracy says that the average instructor "probably brings home 35 percent of what they bring in." This is a very high percentage compared with most businesses. Asked how much you can make in real terms, Tracy would only say that "there is a large gamut of people, from somebody who is doing another job to support this one until it goes, barely making it, trying very hard, beating their head against the wall, and not getting anywhere, to people who are having to find tax shelters and making $8,000 to $10,000 a month." She then adds that "most people are in the middle. They make enough to get by." This is not all bad considering that Jazzercise instructors are only allowed to teach ten hours a week.

**Kinds of Payment Arrangements**

There are other ways that fitness instructors get paid. Some may just get an hourly contract wage which will vary considerably depending on the type of facility they contract with. Municipal governments may only pay $5-$6 an hour, whereas private clubs may pay as much as $12-20 an hour. Another arrangement that is fairly common is a sliding hourly wage which varies according to how many people are in the class. For example, you may receive $8 an hour for up to ten people, $10 an hour for up to fifteen, and $12 an hour for up to twenty. A variation of the sliding scale provides a set hourly rate plus a certain amount per person (such as 20 cents) for every student over some agreed-upon minimum.

**Factors Affecting Income**

These types of payment structures should be negotiated with an eye toward the contingencies and limitations of your work schedule and the facilities in which you teach. Yoga instructor Lori Greenstein speaks of some of these limitations: "The thing with teaching is that you can get really high hourly pay, but you don't work many hours, and you just can't. Say I was trying to do this full time, I would probably be teaching at three different places. By the time I get somewhere, get set up, teach a class, move someplace else, get set up, teach a class, move someplace else, . . . I could probably only do three classes in a day. . . . The best time to offer classes is right after work or in the early evening. There are only so many of those hours per week."

Diedre Szarabajka mentioned a couple of considerations about freelance and drop-in income. If you are renting a space by the hour, you are never really sure whether it may be pulled out from under you, and if you rely on drop-in traffic (as opposed to memberships or session fees) you never know from day to day how many will show up for class. On the other hand, the disadvantage of contracting with just one fitness center, for example, is that your hours are limited. The size of the teaching facility is also a consideration, since you can only squeeze so many people in and still have room to exercise.

Another problem freelance fitness instructors encounter is that facilities only have a limited number of exercise spaces and time frames. As a result, those classes perceived as being specialized often get ostracized to the off hours. If your class is stranded in the off hours realm, it can be difficult to attract the numbers of people to make it profitable to the facility to allow you to change to the peak hours. Patsy Asbury, who teaches stretching classes, often runs into this problem. She is looking for a way out of the bind by teaching classes at her home and other people's homes.

There is money to be made in teaching fitness classes or in owning/operating a fitness center of one sort or another, in spite of the above caveats. There are people who are making a lot of money in these businesses, and there are others who are not — just like in any business. But the key is that the opportunity and potential are there to make as much as you want. You may be like Jody Stock, however, and not really care that much about the money. ''Money was never my number one priority,'' she says. ''All I wanted to do is teach fitness how I wanted to teach it. My first priority is the reputation and being the very best.''

This statement echoes the sentiment of many people who are entering the fitness field. It is not for love of money, but for love of what they do — avocation turned vocation. Lifestyle is the prime determinant more than anything else. Fitness is fast becoming a way of life in America, and as Jody says ''If I can make money at it, I think that's great.''

## DEALING WITH GROWTH

What if you do make money, and what if your clientel keeps growing? What do you do? Where do you go from there? Expansion or franchising may become a real possibility. Bob Farentinos found himself in this position much sooner than he had planned. His membership was growing so fast that he had to either stop selling memberships or expand his facility. His decision to take the expansion alternative was based on his philosophy that it is never a good idea to stop selling memberships and become essentially a closed club.

Diedre Szarabajka, who is presently a contract teacher for facilities other than her own, is thinking of expanding by opening her own fitness center. Not only would this offer more security, it would also offer the chance for growth beyond just increasing the numbers in her existing classes, which becomes infeasible after a point.

As you grow you may find yourself facing what seems like an expansion-stagnation tradeoff, but you should be careful not to expand without a lot of thought, planning, and the financial strength to do so. One of the main causes for the failure of small businesses is that they actually grow too fast, resulting in their cash flow position being taxed beyond its means. Added salaries, overhead, and debt service can mount up fast.

Before expanding you should do the same type of market research as you did for your first business opening. Is your intended market receptive to your product? Jody Stock decided to expand by opening more "Sweat Shops" and found out that people in Kansas City were not as receptive to her operation as those in Colorado. "We're having a little bit harder time in Kansas City because they're not as fitness oriented there. They're like ten years behind here, so maybe I'm in there right at the right time. Either that or I'm stupid — I don't know. It's almost like re-educating the people."

Bob Farentinos has considered opening gyms in other locations and has considered franchising. He is somewhat hesitant, however, because of what expansion will mean for the personality of the gyms. He offers this thoughtful analysis: "At a certain point in time you change. You change . . . with size. You might have one establishment where you are all the time, and it will be more or less the same, but once you delegate that main responsibility, unless you have some really good people who identify with your cause, it's going to change. The other places are going to take on the personalities of the people who are running them, for better or for worse . . . . Since you are selling a service, it's not the same thing as franchising a hamburger fast food place where you are selling the same identical item. . . . You can't sell the same identical service if you have different people selling the service. There are guidelines that they can follow, but all the personalities are different, and a lot of this business is based on personality.''

**The Franchising Option**

As your business prospers you may want to consider selling franchises at some point. Jazzercise, for example, provides the use of its name, experience, organization, and support structure in return for a franchise fee. Those purchasing the franchise are on their own as far as finding space to rent, advertising, and getting students. The main Jazzercise organization does maintain a certain amount of control over the franchise owners, however. As Tracy Van de Boogaard puts it, "there are guidelines with Jazzercise so that you are teaching Jazzercise and not your own program.'' Tracy goes on to explain that "Jazzercise sends us records and a video and written routine sheets. So we have it [and] everybody is doing the same thing . . . . The teachers are all different. We're not little cookie-cutter Judys [Judy Shepard

Misset, the originator of Jazzercise]. We all have our personalities that we put into it, but the routines are the same.''

For some, this may seem stifling to their creativity, for others a welcome relief from the tedious chore of developing routines.

Those buying Jazzercise franchises do not get exclusive areas, but the number of instructors in a given area is limited and the area manager makes sure that different instructors aren't competing by offering classes at the same time around the corner from each other.

Other policies are that all advertising must meet Jazzercise specifications, class size is limited to one hundred students, instructors must pay $70 every two months for the routines, and they are only allowed to teach 10 hours a week.

**Spinoffs**

Another way your business can be expanded is with spinoffs. Many of those interviewed for this book have something going on the side as a direct spinoff of their main activity. This is typical of self-employed people in general, and for this reason it is often difficult to pin anything like a traditional job description on them. The work many of these people do simply evolves with their competencies, and it is not unusual for those who own fitness businesses to also be writers, lecturers, photographers, publicity people, events organizers, or consultants. These sidelines have the added benefit of complementing the main activity and can be a useful source of income during lulls in your workload.

## THE FUTURE

What is the future of businesses which are organized around physical fitness? Jody Stock feels that the current fitness boom is just beginning for two reasons: 1) once people get in shape they never want to get out of shape, and 2) kids in the babysitting services watch their parents exercising and want to join in at a very young age. Thus you have a generation coming up of people highly interested in exercising.

Fitness classes are likely to be popular far into the future, but the question is, how will they change? Exercising once was known as calisthenics. You remember — the huffing and the puffing of situps and pushups to a drill sergeant's cadence. Then music was added in the background and the emphasis started changing from muscle development to aerobic development — i.e., we ran in place for an hour. Dance type movements were added, classes became choreographed, and special clothing designed for aerobics caught on. Jump ropes, Heavy Hands, basketballs, and big screen video replays are now common. Where does it go from here? If you feel you have some insight into that question you'll be strategically poised to take advantage of future opportunities.

# THE EMERGING OPPORTUNITIES IN PHYSICAL FITNESS COACHING

We are all familiar with coaches in our society, but we ordinarily associate them with team sports, athletic clubs and resort companies. The advent of personal fitness coaches, however, is a relatively new development (with the possible exception of a very few coaches catering to extremely wealthy clients).

The growth in demand for personal fitness coaches and the opportunities this represents for individuals seeking self-employment are easily understood. As we grow older most of us no longer have access to coaches because we no longer play on teams. As a result we are left completely on our own for our recreational and fitness needs. We may take a lesson or two in high skill sports such as tennis, racquetball, or skiing, but usually we just blindly leap into a sport or fitness activity, frequently become disillusioned, and move on to try something else. We never seem to reach the skill level we are seeking, we never lose the weight we had hoped for, and we become guilt ridden as a result.

What is wrong here? Why is fitness such an unreachable goal? One reason is the all too prevalent idea that there is a magical route for all of us to develop one stereotypical ideal physique. Fitness programs have been designed to fit some average body-type to a specific program rather than fitting specific programs to each individual.

What is really called for, of course, is just the opposite. We are all unique, with different strengths and weaknesses, and we all need fitness programs which take our unique characteristics into account. As more and more people become educated about fitness, there is a growing demand for this type of specialized training.

Personal fitness coaches provide something very basic that can't be acquired from a book or an aerobics teacher — one-to-one human interaction. Barbara Wakshul has this to say: "There is no substitute for human-to-human interaction, human caring . . . the presence, the true presence of another human being unconditionally present. No book can provide that. . . . It can provide a lot of insight and provocativeness, but it can't provide an almost undefined quality that human-to-human interaction does provide." In order to be able to provide this, a coach "needs to be able to be quiet enough inside to be able to hear where the other person really is and what they really need," Barbara continues.

### Developing Clients' Goals

Barbara's advice is derived from her role as a counselor, not a physical educator, although that does not diminish its applicability. One fitness instructor who takes Barbara's advice to heart is Steve Asher. Steve is in business as a personal fitness coach, and he recognizes that personal interaction is the key which can allow many people to achieve their individual fitness goals. He sees a need for teaching his clients to see results, to be motivated, and to enjoy themselves in accordance with their goals, which he helps them to determine through consultation. "You see people doing things that are wrong," observes Steve. "You ask them 'What is your goal?' What they are doing doesn't fit their goal at all. . . . They are just copying somebody else."

**Motivating Clients To Achieve Their Goals**

Unless goals and activities are compatible and carefully matched, clients will fail to see the results they are seeking and rapidly lose heart and motivation. For this reason Steve, who has a psychology degree, also sees himself in the motivation business. He determines what each person's internal and external motivations are before he designs their fitness program. This marriage of psychology and physical education is necessary in Steve's mind because "psychologists are good at motivating people but don't know about PE; physical educators don't know much about motivating people."

Exactly how does Steve motivate his clients? "Whatever it takes. Some people, you have to pressure them; some people you have to praise and pat and things like that. That's what my job is: to find what that person needs to get motivated."

Another problem in motivating clients is that "some people don't really know that they are getting better." They may be somewhat aware that their endurance is better, for example, but they may need some hard, graphic, and undisputable evidence that they are indeed getting better. This is especially true when people are just starting out and are not in tune with their bodies enough to know whether or not they feel better or are becoming more active and energetic. For that reason, Steve provides charts, graphs, and numbers which map his clients' progress in a variety of different areas. This process is reinforced by individual consultations in which Steve helps his clients become aware of how they feel and what is happening to their bodies.

## Fitness and Finances

Steve's program is designed to appeal to a wide range of financial situations. One of his primary reasons for becoming a personal fitness coach, in fact, was his belief that many people who wanted to become fit couldn't afford to join a club. He also reasoned that some people would prefer to work out in their home environment.

People with widely varying financial resources seek personal fitness coaches. In California there are fitness coaches who drive large vans full of exercise equipment to their wealthy clients' homes at appointed hours. These people want personal coaching without regard to expense. Of course some people want to belong to an athletic club in addition to receiving personal coaching. Steve meets this need by offering a club referral service which recommends different clubs to clients according to their goals, their finances, and their abilities.

## Setting Up a Personal Coaching Business

Personal coaching services vary from very simple to fairly complex arrangements. Tim Adams has three segments to his service. His clients initially fill out a questionnaire concerning vital statistics, disease and injury history, fitness history, exercise preferences, etc. Based on that information, Tim and his client have an initial meeting in order for Tim to "get some idea of what they want to do, where they'd like to be, why they want to do it." Using this information Tim puts together an exercise program consisting of exercise, diet, continual monitoring, updates and consultations. The entire package is designed to provide the information, means and support structure to allow his clients to achieve their goals. Tim added, "I tell them that I won't babysit. If they want to do it, fine. I'll help them, and I'll touch base with them every week."

Steve Asher goes as far as working out with his clients. Often he will "work out with them once or twice a week and give them one time to do it on their own. Then, after the second or third month, I'll go once a week, and then I'll send them somebody else — a student maybe." He also matches up clients with similar goals and abilities so they can work out together. Steve views the services he provides as essentially being a behavior modification program which, given a year to take effect, can become an integral part of his clients' lives.

## Income Potential

Is it possible to make a living by this type of coaching? Tim and Steve think there is a lot of potential, but neither is far enough along for a truly accurate assessment. Tim did coach for about six months as a full-time activity, but stopped because he was only making the equivalent of $12,000 a year. For many people this would be a very acceptable figure for a business that was only six months old, had no real overhead and only required fifty hours a month. Both Tim and Steve charge between $20-25 per hour to start out, but Steve lowers the price as his involvement lessens and he delegates employees to his clients. At this stage he may only charge $10 per hour and pay his employee $6 per hour.

Tim Adams and Steve Asher are basically pioneers in the unexplored territory of personal fitness coaching. The possibilities are really unlimited, and both Tim and Steve are already combining fitness coaching with other interests. Steve has used exercise as therapy for disturbed adolescents, and Tim is thinking of using his techniques as part of a rehabilitation program for drug and alcohol dependency patients. The rationale in both instances is that exercise can improve an individual's self-image and how they feel about themselves overall. Another thing that Tim has looked into is consulting for companies with employee fitness programs. These programs can help employees reduce stress, which in turn helps the company decrease absenteeism and increase productivity.

## EMERGING OPPORTUNITIES IN THE FITNESS HEALTH DISCIPLINES

Personal fitness coaching is definitely one type of emerging opportunity, but it is by no means the only one.

An entire category of emerging opportunities can also be found in the fitness and sports health field. As more and more people have become intensely interested in fitness, our concept of what constitutes good health has undergone a radical transformation. No longer satisfied with merely being free from illness, many Americans have begun defining good health in terms of physical performance.

As concern with physical performance has become increasingly widespread, our language has become peppered with words and phrases once reserved for medical doctors. Now people from all walks of life discuss carbohydrate loading, hypoglycemia, fast- and slow-twitch muscle fiber, and the cardio-vascular benefits of aerobic versus anaerobic exercise.

Unfortunately another group of words have also been bandied about more frequently — words like shin splints, runner's knee, sciatica, tendonitis, and medial-collateral ligaments.

In the rush to become physically fit, many people

have made the mistake of taking a one-dimensional approach and concentrating all their effort on one particular type of physical performance. As people became obsessed with running a certain number of miles per day or week, for example, their legs and feet became overstressed, often leading to injury.

A staggering increase in fitness-related injuries, as well as increased interest in "total wellness" and in injury prevention, has resulted in increased demand for a wide range of fitness-related health disciplines. Among the diverse health disciplines which have responded to this growing demand for specialized fitness services are chiropractic, massage therapy, Aston-patterning, exercise physiology, and physical therapy, as well as certain medical specialties such as podiatry.

## Aston-Patterning as an Example

Many health disciplines are involved in physical fitness, and opportunities in these and related fields are almost certain to continue to grow.

John McConnell provides one example of how an individual can take advantage of the growing opportunities in these fields. John is an Aston-patterner.

To John, an athlete is anyone who wants to use his body in working toward a goal. Through Aston-patterning, John tries to help people realize their goals and not just recover from physical set-backs along the way. He describes what he does in these terms: "It's really a way of changing the functional behavior of the body, so the body itself can perform better, avoid injury, and function in a different way than it usually does. It's really sort of a three-pronged attack. The main mode, the keystone that makes it all really work, in my opinion, is teaching. I spend a lot of time with people teaching them and looking at how they use their bodies in simple activities or athletics or whatever, and getting a sense of how they're using their bodies and how that is limiting performance or creating injury or stopping them from recovering from an injury or whatever the case may be.'' He then works "with ways to replace those stressful movement patterns with ones that provide more ease and more effectiveness.

"And again, there are several parts to that. One is real simple movement patterns that we teach people . . . [for use] as a tool to release stress in certain parts of the body or . . . to integrate one part of the body with another.

"As I continue working with people, the next step is to start integrating those simple tools into activities. A lot of people get really excited because they view injuries or limitations as sort of external things that happen. Like someone says, 'I've been running great for three months and all of a sudden my knee went out.' . . . They really sort of view these as random visitations of external forces. . . . A lot of times we can really begin to remove the mystery of how that is created, what happens to make that occur, and what can be done.''

With that as a capstone, John moves on to the

second aspect of patterning — manipulative work with the structure of the body. This is necessary because although he teaches his clients new movements and makes them more aware of their movements, unconscious old injuries often lock movement patterns into place. Thus a manipulative technique complements the teaching in realigning and rebalancing the body. Both the information and alignment are necessary because, John says, "If you just align them and give no information about what is going on or what's possible, people normally tend to fall back into their old habits."

The final area that John works with involves what he calls the "artifacts that we deal with: shoes and car seats and chairs and tools and bicycles and whatever it might be." He feels that each of these have a significant impact upon the body, and that unless we are able to effectively adapt to such "artifacts," over the long term the patterning will fail.

Patterning was developed by Judith Aston, who had a background in dance, rolfing, and structural patterning. She believed that information and movement, as well as manipulative body work, were necessary and developed what is now known as Aston-patterning on her own. Currently there are only about forty accredited patterners, and that is partly due to the extreme selectivity involved in being chosen for the two-year training program.

Whether or not Aston-patterning has any personal appeal for you, the point to remember is that there is growing demand for all types of fitness- and sports-related health disciplines. There are growing opportunities for self-employment in this emerging field, and if you have the interest and determination it will be worth your while to investigate the many possibilities here.

## SUMMARY

How can you become self-employed in a fitness business of your own? To begin with you need to:

- Research the logistical, organizational, and financial feasibility of your project.
- Target your market.
- Make sure you have enough money to tide you over for awhile.
- Research the strengths and weaknesses of your competition.
- Learn everything you can about the business side of fitness.
- Learn from the mistakes of others.
- Set up policies and rules and adhere to them.
- Train your instructors thoroughly and well.
- Take all necessary legal precautions.
- Advertise and promote your business, keeping in mind that word-of-mouth advertising is the very best kind.
- Have fun!

# Chapter 3
# Opportunities in Travel
# (and Adventure)

Tourism may well become the world's biggest industry by the year 2000. It has averaged a yearly growth rate of over 10 percent since 1960, a rate which indicates that over two billion people will be traveling at the turn of the century. One study, by Herman Kahn and the Hudson Institute, predicts that during the next two decades expenditures for tourism may increase *by a factor of five.*

It is easy to understand the growth of the tourism industry when you consider today's increased leisure time, increased affluence, and cheaper and more efficient modes of transportation. There are a number of other factors, though, which also contribute to the burgeoning growth of this field:

- *There is a growing pool of tourists.* Our society is experiencing a dramatic growth in the number of retirees, for example, with longer life-spans, more financial resources, and a widespread interest in travel. Travel agencies and tour packagers are enthusiastically responding to this and other growth markets.

• *The tourist industry is using computer technology to coordinate reservations world-wide, making travel planning easier and more efficient than ever before.*

• *Governments throughout the world increasingly recognize the economic importance of tourism.* Public policies are often designed to encourage tourism now, and nuisances such as visa requirements are gradually being eliminated.

• *New tourist destinations are opening up.* Mainland China is the prime example, but this is also true of places like Antarctica and parts of the Himalayas.

• *Travel marketing has become much more pervasive and sophisticated.* Besides influencing the choice of destinations, marketing reinforces the idea that travel is the norm for vacations. The idea is subtly conveyed that it is all right to relax and do nothing on your vacation, as long as you go away from home for the experience. If you stay at home on your vacation, on the other hand, you miss out on an important part of life.

• *Communications technology, and especially satellite relays of television broadcasts, constantly increase our awareness of other lands and other cultures.* As our awareness increases, our desire to travel also increases.

• *Finally, the increasingly fragmented, specialized, repetitious nature of modern work contributes to a widely shared feeling that periodic escape is an absolute necessity.*

This last factor, the desire for escape, is the most relevant to our discussion. This chapter won't attempt to tell you how to start a conventional travel agency — other books are available that do a good job of this (see appendix). We are more concerned here with the specialized type of travel which provides the escape so many people are seeking, and that is travel specifically for recreation and adventure.

## THE CHANGING STATUS
## OF ADVENTURERS

Christopher Columbus, adventurer. Daniel Boone, adventurer. Lewis and Clark, adventurers. Adventurers of the past extended the boundaries of civilization, and some were professionals much needed and sought after.

Many of today's adventurers have a somewhat different status in society. They are often called bums now: climbing bums, ski bums, river bums.

You can't help but admire and envy many of these people. Their lives evoke images of a more romantic age — of hard work, communion with the land, dirty hands, and ear-to-ear smiles. There is a bare honesty to their lives, like the rocks they climb or the rivers they run. The problem is that bare honesty often means bare pocketbooks unless, like some of the people you will meet in this chapter, you can find a way to capitalize on your adventuresome spirit.

**Finding Ways to Make Money**

Coral Bowman, a rockclimbing guide and instructor, describes the situation as it relates to rockclimbers. Rockclimbers "get called climbing bums, but in any other circle you'd be considered a professional athlete. But if you're a rockclimber you're a 'climbing bum' because what you're doing is working very little so you can do the thing you love to do. Nobody, still, gets paid directly [for climbing]. . . . You might promote yourself, you might teach, you might do a movie or be in an advertisement. There are ways that you can get money because of who you are in the sport."

We all want to be able to make a living doing the activities that we are best at and like to do the most, but in order to provide a livelihood an activity has to have some demand by the consuming public. Ideally the demand is large enough that other commercial interests (advertisers, television, or equipment manufacturers, for example) can benefit from these consumers also, thereby dramatically increasing the opportunities for all.

This has become the key to making money in adventure/travel activities: You may not make money by simply going out and climbing, rafting, hiking, or whatever, but it may be possible to orchestrate other commercial variables so that your chosen activity can make money for you. Mountain guides in Europe, for example, seem to have taken this to heart. Charlie Fowler, himself a climbing guide, describes the difference: "It's funny, in Europe the guiding scene is really different. The best climbers in European countries are really well known, and they're pretty loaded with money. And the guides over there have the professional status of doctors and lawyers, and they make the same money, too."

In this chapter we will meet a variety of individuals who have learned to turn their love of travel and adventure into a livelihood. We will meet Leslie Bruder, who is the penultimate adventure "bum," and John Harlin, who, in addition to being a climbing and skiing guide, is an adventure lecturer, photographer, and writer. Sandy East and Coral Bowman are climbing guides. Organizing adventure trips is Sarah Larrabee's and Holly Hurtz's specialty, and helping to pay for them is the task of Chris Reveley, founder of the American Mountain Foundation. Darrell

Fralick has a river rafting company, and Dennis and Bailey Stenson take off-road bicycle tours to the tops of mountains.

These people do what they truly like to do best, and they are able to make a living doing it. Leslie Bruder is a case in point. Everything Leslie does typifies the independence of self-employment. Her life is self-sufficient, creative, adventuresome, and innovative, and she learns to deal with new situations as they arise. She is constantly looking for new angles and the cheapest, most effective way to make things happen, and the opportunities she's turned up have taken her around the world guiding, instructing, treking and rafting.

Leslie is in association with four or five trip organizers as an independent consultant. Whenever someone is needed to guide a trek or to be a boatman on a river, Leslie is likely to be called in.

One of the advantages Leslie can offer trip organizers is her personal contacts and connections in a variety of foreign destinations. She has guided week-long tours of the volcanoes of Mexico on three separate occasions, for example, and has managed to establish contacts with local villagers who provide housing for her groups. She does the same thing with houses in Nepal (where she lived for eight months). In addition, she is no stranger to guiding in the Alps, the mountains of Columbia, and other parts of the world.

Leslie is a freelancer in the truest sense of the word. She simply works here and there as needed, without an established business identity of any sort. John Harlin, on the other hand, has a number of different business interests, all related to adventure and travel.

John is a writer, photographer, and lecturer about adventure activities in addition to being the owner and founder of a rockclimbing and cross-country ski guiding business. His biography would read like an adventure novel. He has made ascents and ski descents of peaks in Europe, Canada, the U.S., and Mexico. Other adventures include a 300-mile kayak trip on the Sheenjek River and a six-week exploration of the Konakut River and the Beaufort Sea in the Arctic National Wildlife Range. He has guided climbs in the Utah desert, in Joshua Tree California, of the Grand Teton, and of El Capitan in Yosemite. As owner of Skiing Unlimited, John currently offers guided trips and instruction for both Alpine and Nordic skiers in North America and Europe.

John has this to say about being a climbing guide: "Exploring the vertical world means entering a new dimension in adventure. Your first move lifts you out of the secure flatness of everyday life and into the challenge of a three-dimensional world. This new vertical dimension can be explored safely, but it demands respect. This is why it is so important to learn the skills needed for safe climbing from the best instructors possible. This is also why many people choose to continue using a professional guide even after the preliminary skills have been learned. Strong, competent guides and instructors can open whole realms of the mountain world that would otherwise not be safely approached by most people.''

Coral Bowman, a climbing instructor, is equally enthusiastic: ''Rockclimbing is a wonderful and exhilarating way to enjoy the outdoors. Using the natural features of the rock, placing equipment for protection, the climber combines balance, grace, strength, self-control and relaxation to ascend the rock. It is a dance in a vertical world.

''Stretching our limits, extending ourselves, leads to discovery of new strengths both internal and external. Rockclimbing can be a catalyst for growth — for discovering how we deal with and overcome stress and challenge, translating these experiences to our daily lives. As a vehicle for exploring our issues of trust, fear, vulnerability, and personal and group interactions, rockclimbing is ideal.''

Holly Hurtz, an adventure trip organizer, describes one of her trips in the following terms: ''Our 12-day river expedition through the Grand Canyon gives us a chance to experience first hand the river that is the heart of the west. Such a brief visit is nothing to this immense canyon whose cliffs represent a billion and a half years of geological history. We leave behind the trappings of modern civilization and explore into ages past — often leading to new discoveries about ourselves.''

Darrell Fralik, a whitewater outfitter, emphasizes another aspect of raft trips: ''Part of the raft trip is the actual rafting trip, and then part of it is the comradery that results as you sit around the fire and tell stories about how big the waves were. That doubles the enjoyment people get when they can sit around and share [experiences] with people over a meal and camp out.''

Bailey and Dennis Stenson offer mountain bicycle tours through their company called ''Mystic Wheels'': ''We proudly offer two types of riding tours: on the road and off the road . . . through some of the world's most spectacular scenery — from the Grand Canyon to the Continental Divide in Colorado and Montana. We were raised in this magic land and know its mountainsides, literally, by heart.''

**Travel/Adventure and Self-Growth**

One of the themes that emerge from the above comments is the connection between adventure and self-growth. Holly Hurtz referred to ''new discoveries about ourselves ,'' and Coral Bowman spoke of ''discovering how we deal with and overcome stress and challenge.''

There is no question that experiencing new challenges in a different environment can lead to new perspectives and self-growth, and this is the positive flip-side of the escapism motivation already mentioned. How much you choose to emphasize this self-growth aspect should take into consideration the preferences of the markets you decide to approach.

**Travel/Adventure and Risk**

Adventure means different things to different people. For some, getting out of bed in the morning is an adventure, whereas for others, risking their life is a necessary ingredient for adventure.

For most people, though, adventure refers to experiences which are unusual, exciting, suspenseful, hazardous, or risky. The businesses introduced here strive to provide experiences that are unusual, exciting and suspenseful, but they try at all costs to minimize any hazardous or risky aspects. Holly Hurtz keeps this foremost in her mind when she organizes adventure trips for her clients: "We are morally bound to make sure our people have fun but that they are also safe." Nevertheless, part of the excitement for many people is the perception that under normal circumstances, without their guide, what they are doing would be very risky.

**Travel/Adventure With a Theme**

Is it a problem for tour organizers to come up with trips which can provide the adventure their clients want? Not necessarily, especially when the organizers are seeking adventure for themselves as well. Holly Hurtz says "We're using creative energy to figure out just what we can do [for our clients] and still make it exciting for ourselves." In fact, Holly and her partner, Sarah Larrabee, operate largely on the basis of first deciding where in the world they personally want to go — then they give the trip a theme, make the necessary arrangements, enroll clients and go! The cost of Holly and Sarah's trips are figured into the cost to the customer. That is the reason "Wind Over Mountain" was started in the first place. As Holly tells it, Sarah was suffering from a severe case of "I-want-to-go-around-the-world-itis," and she had to figure out a way to afford it.

By concentrating on creating adventure with a theme, Holly and Sarah have succeeded in providing trips with a unique character. A trip to the Annapurna Sanctuary in Nepal, for example, was organized around a theme of fitness. The trip was guided by a fitness expert who paced the trek and instructed the group in developing stamina, endurance and cardiovascular fitness along the way. The underlying concept was to provide encouragement to people who did not feel fit enough to attempt a Himalayan excursion to try to become fit along the way at a pace that was moderate and supervised. The goal, as Holly describes it, "is not to 'conquer' a mountain, or prove ourselves Olympic athletes but to feel comfortable, happy and accomplished with the challenge of completing a Himalayan walk."

Another Wind Over Mountain trip is "La Tour de France Gastronomique." This is a bicycle trip, and Sarah describes it like this: "For two weeks we'll enjoy the scenery, the pates, and cheeses, the fine cuisine, the auberges or country inns, and the burgandy for which the area is famous. Lest such an excursion lapse into utter decadence, we'll travel from vineyard to vineyard, from auberge to auberge, under our own steam — by bicycle.''

Many Wind Over Mountain excursions are designed to appeal to women. There have been all-women treks to the base of Mt. Everest, raft trips, and a trip to India to "explore the . . . status of women in India and Nepal.'' One raft trip was entitled "A Weekend of Sharing: for Women.'' This theme is described in a flier as follows: "Learning to paddle a raft through whitewater is exhilerating and thrilling. The experience of connecting with one another and learning to work together in a wilderness setting can create strong bonds between individuals. Success depends on cooperation and mutual effort — qualities necessary in any endeavor. This weekend will include time for everyone to share coping skills that have proven effective in creating a supportive environment, and to talk about how their lives are being influenced.''

More challenging raft trips are also offered — through the Grand Canyon on the Colorado River, on the Takshenshini River in Alaska, and on the Rio Bio-Bio in Chile. As you can see, Holly and Sarah believe that adventure can be accessible to individuals at all fitness levels with widely divergent backgrounds and interests as long as the trip is correctly organized and tailored to appeal to a specific market.

**Other Types of Tours**

Holly and Sarah offer hiking, biking, and rafting

trips but the possibilities for combining travel and adventure are virtually limitless. Consider John Harlin's cross-country ski touring business, for example. "Skiing Unlimited: Adventures on Skis" offers a number of weekend and week-long tours in the Colorado Rockies, but also two- to four-week excursions in Europe and volcano climbing and skiing in Mexico. A tour sampling from his brochure looks like this:

Europe
► Two-Week Ski Holiday (with single week option):
► Ski Europe's finest: Chamonix, France and the Valais, Switzerland
► Unlimited skiing — you never repeat a run!
► For the more adventurous: Out of Bounds skiing with a guide
► Stay in comfortable mountain apartments

Four-Week Ski Odyssey:
► The ultimate European skiing experience
► Ski where we want, when we want: Switzerland, Austria, Italy, France — all the Alps!
► Luxury camper-van with shower is our traveling home base.

Haute Route (High Level Route)
► The most famous ski tour in the world
► Traverse the Alps from Chamonix, France

to Zermat, Switzerland
► Excellent huts make every night comfortable

Mexico
► Volcano Climbing and Skiing, Winter Beaching
► Ski from the summits of North America's third and fifth highest peaks — El Pico do Orizaba (18,700 feet) and Popocatepetl (17,900 feet)

John also offers skiing instruction and avalanche courses, and can custom-design a trip to suit individual preferences.

Sandy East and Carl Harrison also offer climbing trips — to Nepal, Great Britain, Alaska and South America — through their International Alpine School. The language used in their tour descriptions is a model of persuasive writing:

"Each day of the 10-day approach will unfold a spectacular variety of scenery. The trail will take us through a series of semi-tropical, rice-growing river valleys, hamlets surrounded by banana trees and terraced hillsides. . . . From here our trail winds its way among the most awe-inspiring mountain scenery in the world. Surrounded by such giants as Ama Dablam (22,494 ft.), Thamserku (22,208 ft.), and Kantega (22,340 ft.) we will make our way up the Khumbu glacier to Everest base camp. . . ."

"We will ascend Kalu Patar (18,500 ft.) for un-paralleled views of 3 of the 4 highest peaks on earth: Everest, Lhotse, and Makalu. . . ."

And in Britain:

"On such routes as Dream of White Horses, you will experience the thrill of climbing with the ocean pounding the wall beneath your feet."

## CONSIDERATIONS IN TRIP PLANNING

### Respect for the Environment

Those leading tour groups have (or at least should have) a special responsibility to their host environments. Bicycle tour guide Dennis Stenson goes out of his way to see that the people on his trips learn to respect the fragile alpine tundra they pass through, and Holly Hurtz is also mindful of this responsibility: "No evidence will be left of our camps on the shore, only footprints erased by the next wind."

With some destinations it is important to emphasize respect for the cultural environment as well as the physical environment.

### Permits

Concern with environmental impact can also be a

legal responsibility. It is necessary to acquire permits issued by the host country to climb in Nepal, for example, and Mt. Everest is currently "booked" all the way until 1990. The permit system is designed both to regulate impact on the terrain and to ensure the safety of climbing expeditions. Arranging for permits is one of the important services offered by tour organizers like Holly and Sarah.

**National Forest Permits**

More important to the outfitter in the United States are the permits required for use of National Forest land. Commercial users of the National Forests are required to get permits even when no overnight use is involved if any of the following criteria are met:

- "The use is an organized feature of a package that a commercial operator offers its guests.
- The use is specifically advertised as a special attraction, the net result of which is that the operator is making specific commercial use of the National Forest.
- In the judgment of the District Ranger, the protection of the National Forest resources warrants the operator to be under permit.
- Any use of the National Forest that returns an income to the operator.
- Examples: Leading or instructing users in outdoor activity, such as hunting, fishing, hiking,

camping, canoeing, boating, mountaineering, horsemanship, ski touring, winter survival, helicopter skiing, and similar types of operations.''

The purpose of this system is to ''insure distribution of commercial operators, eliminate overuse in certain areas and prevent possible conflicts between operators.''

To get a National Forest permit you may be required to supply any or all of the following:

- a statement of need
- estimates of intended use
- confirmation of contact with appropriate rescue groups in the area
- safety and operations plans
- cash or surety bond to guarantee cleanup
- proof that each employee has a valid American Red Cross first aid card
- a copy of your insurance coverage
- copies of your advertising (prior to publication)
- copies of any other licenses that are necessary

## LOGISTICAL PLANNING

Most tours involve a considerable amount of pre-tour planning, which usually involves arranging for food, cooking, sleeping, transportation, and any specialized gear needed.

In addition, each type of tour has its own unique requirements. Trekking, for example, requires work on the logistical problem of pacing the group to reach certain destinations on each day of the trek. Leslie Bruder has her own method of dealing with this: "I sit down with a calender and figure out exactly where I want to be each day, knowing that I could be one or two days off. I tell people to leave at least two days at the end of the trip." Considering the uncertainties of back-country travel, a couple of days of leeway at the end of a trek is definitely a good idea.

# RIVER RAFTING AS AN EXAMPLE OF LOGISTICAL PLANNING

Like any other type of travel/adventure business, river rafting requires careful organizing and planning. Attention to details can mean the difference between a trip that goes off perfectly and a trip that becomes an absolute disaster.

Darrell Fralick is only too aware of this. "I really enjoy the river. I really enjoy the time spent on the river," he says, but he goes on to qualify his statement. "I'll tell you, there's a hell of a lot of work getting it all together."

### River Permits

Because of the lead time involved, arranging for permits will need to be one of your first steps in planning river raft trips. If you don't have a concession for one river that you can continually use, you should plan your trips back to back on different rivers for maximum efficiency. Unless you can make the back-to-back permit arrangements, you'll most likely be faced with large amounts of "down time" between trips. Arranging for permits right in a row will require patience, planning, and time, and your best bet is to start working on getting your permits as soon as you have some definite trips in mind.

## Equipment

After you've made your permit arrangements and gotten your tour group together (see "Reaching Your Market" below) you'll need to prepare an equipment list for each person telling them what they should bring. Your own equipment list will need to be detailed and extensive since you are the outfitter as well as the organizer and guide.

You'll need to plan ahead to load your bus (old school buses work well for this purpose) and your trailer with the necessary rafts, oars, food, cooking equipment, pumps, life jackets, first aid supplies, etc. You may need room for transporting people with your bus too, or you may be able to meet your group at a prearranged destination near the "put-in" point.

## Transportation and Shuttles

Since there is a put-in point on the river, there

will naturally have to be a "take-out" point as well, and this presents the problem of somehow re-uniting your tour participants with their cars.

When Darrell started his company he had trouble explaining to his clients that after a long drive to the put-in point they would have to drive even further to leave their cars at the take-out point. "They drive all the way up there" — to a point on the Salmon River in Idaho in this case — "20 hours, and they get there about two in the morning. . . . They fall out of the car and we say, 'Okay, we've got to get the drivers together to drive a shuttle. We're going to drive all the cars to the other end, and we're going to come back in the van.' " It was an eight-hour trip each way.

Most people would prefer to pay more and have a vehicle waiting at the other end. Now Darrell leaves a day or two early and shuttles vehicles himself. Another alternative — one Darrell considers a luxury — would be to have a driver shuttle vehicles while the party is on the river, and in some situations a shuttle by airplane can be justified.

## CALCULATING YOUR COSTS

Cost considerations are closely related to logistical considerations because planning often involves making trade-offs between time, effort and expense.

The equipment costs for a river rafting business, to continue with our example, can be substantial. If you are willing to substitute time and effort for money (by planning your purchases carefully and opting for used equipment that may need repairs, for example) you can nevertheless start on a small scale without a major capital investment.

Darrell Fralick's initial outlay was about $10,000, which is certainly reasonable considering what he was able to acquire with the money: three rafts, a 24-passenger bus, two trucks, pumps, life jackets, oars/paddles, cooking gear, waterproof bags, and a first aid kit. Please note that we are talking about equipment costs only here. Any type of tour business will also incur operating costs such as advertising, repairs, phone service, food, gasoline, and employees or contract labor.

In the case of rafting operations this last item — contract labor — can be a substantial expense. Unless you choose to operate what is essentially a one-raft operation, you'll need to hire boatmen for your trips. There are a number of people who make livings as boatmen, going from river to river and job to job. Darrell usually hires three for each trip, and typically he will pay them $300 each for a six-day trip.

**Cash Flow**

Naturally boatmen want to be paid in cash at the end of the trip, and this raises the question of cash flow. It's not enough simply to be concerned about taking in more money than you pay out — you must also make sure you have enough cash on hand to meet your obligations as they come due. Failure to plan for your cash flow (including contingency plans for emergencies such as equipment breakdowns) can ultimately destroy your business, even though it may be growing at a healthy rate.

Darrell's way of dealing with the cash flow problem is to make every effort to get his money "up front" before the trip begins. He insists on a 50 percent deposit when the reservation is made and tries to get the entire fee at that time. An otherwise profitable trip can quickly be turned into a losing proposition by "no shows," with predictable effects on your cash flow situation.

**Other Expenses**

Every type of tour will have unique costs, especially with regard to equipment. Dennis and Bailey Stenson require a sagwagon (support vehicle), a bike trailer, and bicycles or arrangements for bicycle rentals. Climbing operations need climbing equipment such as ropes, chocks, carabiners, and safety helmets.

Some costs are shared by all types of travel operations, however. Most of these businesses will require insurance which, in the case of a climbing operation, might cost $600 a year based on 100 client-days. Coral Bowman has found it necessary to employ an office manager at peak times, and at the very least you will need a phone answering machine or an answering service. In addition there will be expenses for printing, advertising, stationery, and office supplies. If you plan to do promotional mailings to prospects and previous clients, as most tour operators do, you'll need to budget money for that, too. Holly Hurtz spends $2,000-3,000 a year on mailings alone.

One other expense category we should mention involves your own travel to investigate destination points prior to putting a tour together. Those signing up for a trip naturally expect you to have some first-hand familiarity with your destination, and the only way to effectively make local contacts and plan tour routes is to spend the time and money to experience an area in some depth yourself. The more trips you make to a given area the better your tours will tend to be (unless you become so bored you can no longer work up any enthusiasm for the trip).

## PRICING

Considering the expenses mentioned above, pricing your services correctly is imperative. Although you definitely should find out what competing services are charging for your particular activity, it's important not to base your pricing solely on what your competition is charging.

An equally important consideration may be the characteristics of the particular market you have decided to target. Some clients may be perfectly willing to pay 30 percent more than what your competition is charging, for example, to go first class. Conversely, there may be a vast market for cut-rate services not currently being offered.

In very general terms, the tendency in these types of travel and adventure businesses has been to undercharge rather than overcharge. Some recreation entrepreneurs have trouble realizing that what is a day-to-day life for them is the consumate vacation for others, and that those planning their dream vacations are often willing to pay extra for assurance that their vacation will meet their expectations.

## Economies of Scale

As with most other businesses, there are economies of scale which can be realized in these recreation businesses. This simply means that, within a given range, your costs per unit of service will go down as you serve more people.

To understand how this works it is helpful to distinguish between fixed costs and variable costs. Fixed costs remain the same regardless of how many clients you serve and include start-up costs for going into business (having stationery designed and printed, opening a business bank account, etc.), your investment in equipment, and many of your administrative and promotional expenses.

Variable costs increase according to the number of people you serve, and include any supplies which are consumed, temporary employees or subcontractors, and equipment rentals.

Rafting provides an instructive example. Given the basic rates you charge for your service, do you want to have a one-, two-, or three-raft company? Depending upon how many customers you can attract and how frequently you can attract them, the more rafts you have the more money you will make. Some people don't see this because they only see their costs increasing as they buy more rafts. Apart from the actual investment in rafts and accessories, however, which is a one-time expense, the other costs of organizing raft trips remain relatively fixed whether you are taking one raft or five. For example, transportation to and from the river is one of your biggest operating expenses, and this will probably be the same for one raft or five. The same goes for much of the time and money spent organizing the trip. So, as these fixed costs are distributed over more customers, the cost of providing the service to each additional customer goes down.

Your variable costs will increase with each additional customer, but as you buy in larger quantities you can often realize substantial savings. If you are buying food for large groups at a time, for example, you may be able to buy some items wholesale.

**Staffing for Peak Periods**

Short-term labor costs are another variable expense which must be considered. An additional boatman is required for each additional raft, for example, at a cost of $50-75 per day.

Coral Bowman explains how paying an additional climbing guide makes economic sense in her operation. Except for the original investment in more equipment, which is paid back after a certain amount of time, the costs of organizing a trip are the same whether she takes three or six people. The only cost that doesn't go down or stay the same is the cost of a second instructor to teach the other three people. But if each of these clients is paying $100 and Coral is paying the instructor $150, she is grossing an additional $150 by increasing the size of the trip. This $150 has to cover the additional variable costs that accrue as a result of each additional person added to the trip, but for a one-day climb this may only involve the cost of food, with the rest of the money becoming net profit.

**Large or Small Groups?**

In general, if there is a choice to be made between large and small trips you will make more money with the larger trips. Much depends upon your management and cost control abilities, however, and on the amount of demand for your services. Having the capability of running raft trips for several dozen people does you no good unless you can fill the rafts fairly consistently. Making a reasonably accurate assessment of the demand you can expect — before investing in expensive equipment — is obviously important. Starting small and expanding only in response to additional demand is usually the best strategy.

**Length of Your Trips**

Another factor to consider in setting your prices is the length of the trips you plan to offer. Many people in the rafting business prefer longer trips for the security of knowing the rafts are full for that specified period of time. There are trade-offs, however, because if you are successful in filling your rafts for one-day trips you may make more money because you can charge more for the one-day trips.

Generally speaking your expenses are higher for the one-day trips, too, because some of the expenses (such as transportation), which are one-time costs for multi-day trips, are encountered every day with one-day trips. Your fee for a multi-day trip will figure out to be less per person per day than for a one-day trip, but since your costs are probably less you may find that you can make more of a net profit on the longer trips. To find out which approach is more profitable for your particular operation you will need to keep careful income and expense records and compare your net profit figures for different types of trips.

Along with deciding what length of trip you want to offer you will need to consider the number of customers and the type of customers you are offering your service to. If you're operating a river rafting operation, for example, and business is likely to be slow during the week, you might try to take five to ten people on a five-day trip and then take ten to twenty people on one-day trips Saturday and Sunday.

Weekend trippers are often a completely different type of clientel from those signing up for week-long trips. Weekenders are more likely to be beginners, and they may sign up on an impulse without really having an interest in rafting. Those taking extended trips, on the other hand, are likely to be more experienced rafters who have planned a vacation around the trip. Each type of trip should be marketed differently to reflect these differences in clientele.

## REACHING YOUR MARKET

The key to reaching your market in the travel and adventure business, as in any other business, is to focus your efforts on your targeted customer group. You must try to imagine your average customer in as much detail as possible, and try to understand what unique characteristics your customers share. Most importantly, you must understand what motivates this type of individual to purchase services like yours.

You should be as specific as possible in focusing your marketing efforts on the particular market you've decided to target. You can learn from the example of Susan Eckert in this regard. Susan founded Rainbow Adventures, Inc. because she felt that women over 30 were interested in wilderness trips but that inexperience kept them from taking such trips on their own.

Aiming her marketing efforts at just this group — inexperienced outdoorswomen over the age of thirty — Susan launched her business. According to an article in *Venture* magazine, 110 women took part in twelve trips during Susan's first summer in business, and 300 signed up for trips during her second year. Her start-up costs were about $15,000, and this included expenses for insurance, legal and accounting fees, promotional expenses, and the cost of setting up an office.

Among the 22 trips currently offered are a $695 white-water raft trip in Utah, $195 weekend cross-country ski trips in Wisconsin, and a $1,995 two-week camel safari in Kenya.

Susan sets her prices at 40 percent above her costs, and she expects to open another office within two years. Her business is clearly doing well, although it's only two years old, and if there's a lesson to be learned from Susan's experience it is this: Don't try to be everything to everybody. Instead, focus your marketing efforts on a specific customer population.

**Direct Mail Promotion**

Practically speaking, most people in the travel/ adventure business find that various sorts of mailings to previous and prospective clients are their most effective marketing tool. Although it is possible to rent mailing lists of people with almost any interest imaginable, mass mailings to a rented list can be prohibitively expensive for those just starting out. Generating your own list from friends, contacts, and past customers may be an affordable alternative. In just this way, Holly Hurtz and Sarah Larrabee have generated a 5,000-person list. Darrell Fralick and Sandy East have put their own lists together, too, and use the lists to "cultivate" their clients. This is a cumulative effort in that each communication which goes to receptive clients becomes reinforcing.

Sarah and Holly send newsletters to the people on their mailing lists. A great deal of thought goes into making the letters enjoyable to read as well as informative in introducing upcoming tours. The following letter is an excellent example of combining these two aims:

Dear Kashmir Trekker:

The enclosed itinerary is for a unique Himalayan adventure which combines Moghul-style trekking with leisurely houseboat life and an overland excursion to remote Ladakh, which opened its doors to foreigners in 1976.

In Kashmir the Himalayas put on their most gracious aspect, with gentle foothills covered in pine and fir, watered by delightful trout-filled streams, inhabited by nomadic shepherds, and surrounded by snowy giants. Jehangir, the Moghul ruler of India from 1599 to 1627, said of his pleasure gardens there:

If ever on Earth there was a Paradise of Bliss,
It is this, It is this, It is this!!!!

Because of its mild summer climate, with no monsoon, and its geography, Kashmir is the perfect Himalayan destination during July and August. It also suits people of varied trekking experience. We decided to provide luxury trekking here for a taste of how the Moghul emperors and their British successors used to move around the mountains. We'll have walk-in tents with folding cots, sinks with running water, a fully stocked bar, and hopefully a hot tub!!! Trekking days will be fairly easy and short, so you'll have plenty of time for fishing and photography or, for the enthusiastic, side hikes and climbs. Ponies will be available for those who prefer to ride part of the way. Trout are plentiful here: streams were stocked by British sportsmen and fish is not part of the local diet.

Ladkah, also known as Little Tibet, is the only place where Tibetan religion and lifestyle have continued uninterrupted by social and political upheaval. Until recently, it has had little contact with the West. This is a unique opportunity to participate in such a culture, elegant and dignified in its simplicity.

The cost of this luxury trek is $1995,

which includes all room and board except meals in Delhi, all surface transportation and transfers, houseboats and sightseeing in Srinagar and Ladakh, tented accomodations and full service during the trek including pack ponies, cooks, guides and bearers. We'll provide all necessary special cooking equipment but avid anglers are advised to bring their own poles, etc. If you wish to participate in this adventure, please return the enclosed application along with a nonrefundable $300 deposit. You will be billed for the remainder in May and for the airfare (sample airfare $1260 NY-Delhi-NY) in June. We'll also send a detailed equipment list, reading list and other information. If you have any questions, give us a call.

Happy Trails!!!

**Promoting to Travel Agents**

Working through travel agents can be an effective way of promoting your business if you're willing to pay a commission on the clients the agents sign up. Holly Hurtz feels that this approach works for their operation, and she is currently branching out by advertising in travel industry magazines in order to reach more agents.

Another approach would be to use direct mail to promote to travel agents. You could rent mailing lists for this purpose, or you could create your own list by going through directories available at the library. It's probably not a good idea to use the same promotional material for travel agents that you are using for consumers because these are two separate markets with different motivations. Your promotional materials to the travel agents, for example, should emphasize the profitability of signing up clients for your tours.

**Advertising in Sports Magazines**

Dennis Stenson found that advertising in *Bicycling Magazine* was expensive — but it was so effective that a few initial ads have provided all the customers necessary (along with repeat customers and word of mouth) for his business. Darrell Fralick, on the other hand, doesn't advertise because "I don't think it is cost effective for my operation."

If you want to try advertising your business, consider testing less expensive ad media initially. Try a variety of different ads and keep careful records of which ads produce the best results. "Keying" your ads (by adding a different department number to your address for each ad, for example) simplifies this process, but you should also get in the habit of always asking new clients where they heard about your business. Don't go to larger-sized ads or more expensive media until you're certain the ad you want to run has a good chance of at least breaking even.

**Publicity**

Publicity is essentially free advertising provided by the news media because you have a story they think their readers will be interested in. The trade-off is that you have very little or no control over what the media will say in their coverage of your particular story.

Press releases are your major tool for tapping into free publicity about your organization. There is a standard format which your press releases should conform to:

- Double space your release on your letterhead.

- Keep it brief and concise — preferably one page, no more than two.

- Summarize your message in a short headline ("Maverick Tours Announces Plans for South American Adventure Trip").

- On the upper right side of the page give the date you would like the story to run ("For Immediate Release" or "For Release Sept. 30").

- Under the release date give the name and phone number of a contact person who can be called for clarification or additional information.

- Put your most important facts in the first couple of paragraphs. (If the paper is short on space they'll probably cut your release from the bottom.)

- Take care to send your release to the right person, and if you don't know who that person is, call first to find out.

Coral Bowman has had tremendous success by sending out press releases announcing the courses offered by her climbing school. The releases have been included in news features and blurbs in newspapers and magazines, and have led to both magazine and television interviews for Coral. Coral feels that part of her success is due to the orientation of Great Herizons to women, which may make it more newsworthy than some other climbing schools.

Sandy East has also had success with publicity, however. He reports that the summer business of his climbing school increased 30-40 percent after an article on the school was published in *Sportstyle* magazine. Learning to prepare effective press releases can be an extremely worthwhile effort.

As with advertising promotion, you'll need to know which of your publicity efforts are paying off and which aren't. Asking new clients how they found out about you should become an ingrained habit for both you and your employees.

**Promoting to Companies**

Darrell Fralick has found that promoting his rafting service to companies can be effective. Many companies have an individual who acts as a recreational director in organizing and coordinating company functions, and this is the person you will need to seek out and develop an ongoing relationship with. In this way you only have to deal with one person instead of each member of the group you're putting together, and this can save time, hassles, and ultimately, money.

## FINDING YOUR OWN NICHE

People get started in the travel/adventure business in a variety of different ways. For some, the businesses begin as hobbies that gradually seem to take on a life of their own. For others, a sudden inspiration is responsible.

Chris Reveley's experience is typical of the sudden inspiration group. His organization, the American Mountain Foundation (AMF), differs from the others in this chapter because it is non-profit, but the principles are basically the same.

As Chris describes it, the origin of his idea for the AMF came about like this: "I was lying in bed one night, and I was angry about the unavailability of sponsorship for expeditions, and I sat up in bed and said, 'Well, why isn't there just another organization to provide sponsorship?' And my wife said, 'just make one yourself and shut-up and go back to sleep.' I said 'okay, okay,' and that's what we did.''

The result of this conversation was the AMF, which was established to ''encourage, support, and promote American mountaineering.'' Basically the AMF has three separate functions: to disseminate information, provide financial assistance, and offer educational programming. The information aspect includes providing referrals and information on mountain routes, other climbers, and transportation to the mountains. The financial assistance aspect involves seeking donations as a tax-exempt, fund-raising organization and overseeing the distribution of the funds, and the educational aspect includes providing programs for schools on mountaineering. Part of the rationale for this last function, as Chris sees it, is to ''give kids a chance to see an alternative to football.''

Coral Bowman's business didn't begin with this type of sudden inspiration. Her business gradually evolved out of her hobby of rockclimbing. It all started by taking a few friends climbing now and then, then giving some beginners a few pointers, and it just kept growing to the point she realized she was in business and should be charging money for what she was doing.

As Coral's business continued to evolve, she operated like many businesses in the early stages — ''from crisis to crisis.'' What helped her get through this period was a conscious commitment: ''When I started, I made a five-year commitment. . . . I'm going to do this for five seasons and take it as far as I can get it, and at that point I can reassess whether it's meeting my needs in the way I want it to."

For other people, making a conscious commitment to the business is not really necessary. For Darrell Fralick it was all a very simple matter. He started his rafting company "just because it's part of my life I didn't want to give up." He realized that if he was going to go rafting 60 days a summer, he should be making money at it.

## POSSIBLE DRAWBACKS

Every type of business has its drawbacks — even a business combining fun, excitement, adventure, and travel. Holly Hurtz and Sarah Larrabee have been conducting about five trips a year for nine years through their company and have learned that world travel can interfere with a stable home life. Holly puts it this way: "Neither of us wants to be out of the country for six months because we have our lives that go on here in spite of everything that we do. And you know, one of the things that you give up if you are constantly traveling is any kind of long-term relationships, and that's a big thing to be willing to give up."

Other possible drawbacks include long hours, burnout, and the seasonal character of most outdoor travel businesses. Because there is pressure to take full advantage of a short season, long hours are common and burnout can easily result, even when the work involves a favorite activity.

Finally there is the risk of accidents and resulting liability. The risk of accidents and injury is always present to a certain degree in these businesses, and beyond having the necessary first aid credentials and insurance, there is not much you can do. You can ask your clients to sign waivers releasing you of liability, but ultimately you have to learn to live with a certain amount of risk.

Coral Bowman feels that having a partner or someone else you can rely on relieves the pressure, especially on extended trips, and speaks of the "comic relief" such a person can provide. Darrell Fralick agrees that you need somebody you can rely on and talk to. "A lot of times you get to a rapid, and you're three days out somewhere — you want to have some support. You don't want to look around and see a lot of people who have never been there before."

Unless, of course, you consider *that* an adventure!

# Chapter 4
# Opportunities
# in Sporting Goods

The overall growth in recreation spending is clearly reflected in sales of all types of sporting goods. From scuba gear to backpacks and from running shorts to canoe paddles, sporting goods are selling like never before.

Within the general category of sporting goods, fitness equipment is a particularly bright spot. One study of the sporting goods market produced by Frost & Sullivan, the marketing consulting organization, predicts a 13 percent infation-adjusted annual growth rate for fitness equipment through the mid-1980s.

Among the retailers Frost & Sullivan surveyed, "Exercise/physical fitness equipment was the second most frequently listed strong growth product area." The first most frequently listed? Windsurfing and sailboarding.

Reasons cited for the growth in fitness equipment sales include a significantly larger number of women now interested in fitness, more older people becoming fit today, and growth of sales to the younger age group market as families become increasingly fitness-conscious.

## SPECIALTY RETAILING

"Sporting goods" is an extremely broad category which includes activewear apparel as well as specialized equipment for a wide variety of sports and the growing subcategory of fitness equipment. There is a definite trend toward specialty stores in sporting goods retailing today. For this reason — and also because a retail operation carrying a full range of sporting goods often requires a larger capital investment than most people can easily handle — this chapter will only consider opportunities in specialty sporting goods retailing.

### Starting on a Shoestring

Gary Neptune, owner of Neptune Mounaineering, offers one example of starting a specialized sporting goods store without a major capital investment. Unlike many retail operations Gary opted to grow at a carefully controlled rate, never overburdening himself with inventory or over-extending himself financially.

Many retail businesses today seem unwilling to

pay as they go. "I have never operated that way," Gary says, "and it probably means that I went an awful lot slower. It's a real conservative way to do it. But then again, everything that is here is mine, and I don't owe anybody anything. And if I have a bad year, it's not going to wipe me out like it could somebody with a lot of bank financing." As a result, Gary has arrived at a point where he "can relax a little bit more." He then adds, "I think I am beyond the point of making one serious error that will run me out of business."

Things were not always so secure for Gary, however. Looking back he says "I made lots of mistakes and made up for them with hard work and persistence." He always tried to keep the business simple so he could learn by trial and error on a scale that he could handle. This was important because, as Gary says, "for the first five years or so, I was always almost out of business." If anything went wrong in those first few years, it could have ruined him — he just did not have the money to survive a seriously wrong decision, miscalculation, or a bad year. At one point in the beginning when his store wasn't doing well, his father offered to bail him out and send him back to graduate school. Gary recalls that he "thought real hard about it, because not many people get an easy way out of a big mistake like that. I thought about it and basically decided I liked what I was trying to do, and I still thought that there was hope, so I stuck with it and I'm glad I did."

**Importance of Specializing**

Gary feels that specializing (in mountaineering equipment, for example) is important for a small retail sporting goods business. A lot of specialty shops "get too big and then they're not specialty shops anymore," he says. One problem with diversification is finding people who are sufficiently qualified in diverse sports to be your salespeople. Another problem is maintaining a special uniqueness and ambience for your shop: "You might have departments and specialty departments, but then each would lose touch of the others, and you'd lose a certain flavor. . . . We like it the way it is."

Sports Arena Ltd. is another example of a specialty approach to retailing sporting goods. This unique Chicago-based firm sells official jackets, caps, and jerseys worn by major league football, baseball and hockey teams. The company buys their merchandise from manufacturers who pay a royalty fee to the leagues.

There appears to be a good future in this type of business. Licensed sports products will bring in $1 billion in retail sales in the 1980s according to *Sporting Goods Dealer*, a trade publication. Sports Arena Ltd. now has four stores and is planning to franchise their concept in the very near future. People seem willing to pay a premium to wear official major league uniforms — a St. Louis Cardinals baseball shirt, for example, retails for about $50.

### Specialization by Sex

Most specialty sporting goods stores focus on a particular type of sport, but stores carrying sporting goods specifically for women are now catching on.

Sporting goods stores for women make good sense. There has been an explosive growth in women's athletics in the last 10 to 15 years, along with expansions in school sports for girls mandated by the federal government. Many of the general sporting goods stores carrying some lines of women's products are not able to provide the kind of advice women want — especially women who are just becoming involved in an activity that is new to them.

Stores such as New York's "Sporting Woman" are springing up to fill this need. With equipment, shoes and clothing for exercise, aerobic dance, racquetball, running, tennis, swimming and other sports, the store has a wide assortment of merchandise. Matt Zale and Ron Greenberg, who launched the business in 1981, have made a deliberate effort to achieve a balance between fashion and function in their activewear, thereby appealing to both serious and casual "sporting women."

### Specializing in Consignment Goods

Probably the most inexpensive approach to starting a retail sporting goods business is to open a consignment shop.

"Sports Again" is one such shop. It was opened

with an initial investment of about $3,000 by Liv Diaz and Deborah Patten, who built their original inventory by attending garage sales and flea markets. Once their shop opened for business people brought in their used sporting goods equipment to be sold on consignment.

Most items are sold on a straight 50/50 percentage, although a somewhat better percentage is given consignees for items valued over $150. The price is set according to how much was originally paid for the item, the current retail value of similar products, and the popularity and condition of the item.

Sports Again is now expanding into new but discounted sportswear, and occasionally the shop will buy used equipment outright (if someone is leaving town, for example, and would rather not bother with a consignment sale). Samples bought from sales reps are still another source of inventory, and these are sold at reduced prices like everything else in the store.

According to an *In Business* article, the owners are very pleased with the way business is going. Liv Diaz feels that similar stores can expect to generate $7,000 to $10,000 a month in sales.

# THE NUTS AND BOLTS OF RETAILING

**Investment Requirements**

The actual amount you will need to invest

depends on the type of store you're planning, your own experience and ability, and the market where you are located. The following operating expense ratios for an "average" sporting goods store were provided by the National Sporting Goods Association (NSGA) and may help you with your planning.

Operating expenses ratios
expressed as a percentage
of net sales

| | |
|---|---|
| Cost of goods sold: | 67.0 |
| Gross profit: | 33.0 |
| Wages: | 13.6 |
| Rent: | 2.3 |
| Advertising: | 2.0 |
| Total expenses: | 28.8 |

You will probably need to acquire enough capital to carry your operation through a minimum of two to three years of operation. Many large retail firms feel that three to four years are required for a new store to return a profit. Cash flow will be critical because without sufficient cash coming into the business it will not be possible to take advantage of good buys from vendors or to pay invoices during the cash discount period.

**Profitable Operating Practices**

A study of retail success in nine Illinois communities set up the following criteria for measuring the success of a store: (1) rate of employee growth, (2) rate of increase in the owner's investment, (3) rate of return on the investment, and (4) rate of return on sales. Using these considerations, the study analyzed 419 retailing firms to determine the operating practices associated with success. Here are the major findings:

- Successful stores encourage salespeople to increase their sales by organized methods.

- Successful retailers add new items more frequently than others.

- Successful retailers conduct more special sales and are especially active in community promotion campaigns.

- Successful retailers advertise more consistently in newspaper display columns.

- Successful retailers maintain more frequent and detailed merchandise and operating data, but depend on their accountants to collect them.

- Successful retailers are better educated, are well informed about their firms' financial data, and are aggressive yet friendly.

Many small retailers have tended to accept the economic role of being distributing agents for manufacturers and wholesalers. While such a restricted role may serve local customers' needs for convenience goods, it will not assist growth or the ability to attract from a wide trading area. If you intend for your store to grow you must identify yourself as a purchasing agent for your selected customer market. You must determine your customers' needs and then select from the mass of competing products on the market whatever assortment best meets those needs. Independence of manufacturer domination can be a distinguishing feature of your store. This doesn't mean that you will stop promoting national brands and cooperating in the conduct of joint promotion plans. However, your decisions won't be based on a supplier's insistence but rather upon your own conviction that such association will best serve your *customers'* interests.

**Choosing Your Location**

There's an old saying that three things are necessary for a retail business to succeed: location, location, and location.

While it's certainly true that location is a critical factor, it may also be true that location in the most high-rent area of town is not necessary for your particular type of business. If you're planning to open a bicycle shop, for example, and want to target the college market, you may be able to find a much less expensive location away from downtown but closer to your local college campus. The important point to remember is that you want to locate where you can best attract your anticipated clientele.

Another factor to consider when choosing your location is the amount of impulse buying, compared to regular repeat customers, you expect to have. If you stock highly specialized equipment not otherwise readily available and can build a loyal repeat customer base, the kind of location necessary for impulse buying may not be necessary for your business.

Parking facilities either nearby or adjacent to your location are essential for almost any shop. Front display windows may or may not be important, depending upon the type of store you are considering. An added plus for any location would be room for expansion in future years.

Before signing a lease you should compare rental rates in different parts of town. Keep in mind that the least expensive rent is not necessarily your best bet. Focus on the particular market you are targeting, and ask yourself what kind of location would be most convenient and appealing to this particular group.

You will have to negotiate the term of your lease, the services which are to be provided by the landlord, and the extent of your responsibilities as a tenant. An agreement will have to be reached on who is responsible for any remodeling, painting, rewiring, or other improvements. Termination clauses and subleasing arrangements should be clearly understood and spelled out, and it's a good idea to have an attorney review the lease contract before you sign it.

## Your Store's Image

Some general sporting goods stores are fairly successful because they have a convenient location. Situated along major traffic arteries or in shopping centers, they get much of their patronage from customers who find it quicker and easier to buy there than to go somewhere else. But specialty sporting goods stores must develop distinct, favorable characteristics that customers will associate with them.

When customers decide to go shopping (as distinguished from going to buy tennis balls or other staples) they are apt to mentally check off the stores in the shopping area that are most likely to carry just what they are looking for and that offer the kind of service they prefer. They have a mental image of the competing stores in their communities, based on their experiences and observations, the experiences of friends, store advertising, etc.

### Factors That Shape Image

Your store's image will probably depend upon the following factors:

- The nature of your merchandise line or lines.

- The size of your market. You must find in your trading area a sizable group of customers interested in the combination of merchandise and service that you will offer.

- The strength of your competition. Ideally, your store will cater to a group of customers whose merchandise and service requirements are not being satisfactorily met by your competitors.

- Personal and staff capability.

- Capital availability. Building a store image is limited to the amount of capital available for this purpose, and wide assortments, best quality, and an opulent store atmosphere will require more capital than many new retailers can readily command.

Even with limited capital there are some things you can do to project your store's image. You can select two or three features in which your store has the capacity to excel and then place major emphasis on developing them and making your community aware of them. Moreover, you should identify customer groups from your community that have certain common merchandise and service interests and try to adjust your store's personality to their needs and wants.

*Interior Display*

In recent years, tremendous advances have been

made in interior display. Self-service fixtures have largely replaced the old enclosed type. You'll want to give careful attention to the selection of modern fixtures that fit in with your store's interior scheme. Many of your suppliers can provide fixtures, at nominal cost, designed to display their lines. If you use them, take care that they fit into your overall scheme; otherwise, they will look out of place.

Your product arrangements are even more important than your fixtures. Here are some generally recognized ideas that will help you plan attractive, efficient self-service layouts:

- Put impulse goods near the front of your store, and intersperse them with demand products so that as many people as possible will see them.

- Think about which shopping goods the customer would have in mind before entering the store and place them in areas that receive less traffic and where impulse and convenience lines must be passed to reach them.

- Frequently change "ends," special displays set at the end of counters that are readily observable from many points in the store.

- Locate and arrange your stock so that customers are drawn toward the side of the store and then toward the rear. (You want to create a circular traffic pattern that exposes customers to at least a third of the entire assortment before they leave the store.)

- If you carry competing brands in various sizes, give relatively little horizontal space to each item, and make use of vertical space for the different sizes and colors. This exposes customers to a greater variety of products as they move through the store.

- Avoid locating impulse goods directly across the aisle from demand items that most customers are looking for. If you don't, the impulse item may not be seen at all.

- Make use of vertical space through tiers and step-ups, but be careful to avoid much above eye level or at the floor. The area of vertical vision is limited.

**Dealing With Key Suppliers**

In trying to carry a wide and varied assortment, many small merchants spread their buying among too many suppliers. They don't buy enough from any one source to make their store's patronage important to the seller. As a result, they fail to get the special prices, service, and promotional opportunities offered to others. For best results, select your suppliers very carefully from among those with wide product lines. Then you will get good treatment and your assortments will be wide enough to satisfy your customers' wants.

As a small retailer you will probably lean heavily on your wholesalers, because they can quickly provide you a variety of merchandise in small lots, if necessary, with prices and terms comparable to those of the manufacturer. Your wholesalers also assume the responsibility of forecasting your requirements long in advance, and this gains you greater inventory turnover.

The margin that the wholesaler exacts is usually a small price to pay for his valuable services. In activewear fashion lines, however, direct contact with appropriate manufacturers is preferable because the timing of the new styles is of critical importance.

*Vendor Relations*

It's essential to maintain cordial and mutually profitable relationships with your vendors. Arbitrarily canceling orders, returning properly delivered goods, and taking unearned discounts injure the buyer as well as the seller. A store that has been unfair in its dealings is not going to get special promotional offerings and extra services. You should personally approve all cancellations and returns to vendors. You should also make it a policy to see all salesmen who call; if you do, you won't be guilty of favoritism, and you won't overlook profitable buying opportunities. At the same time, watch out for tricky suppliers that substitute, cut quality, discriminate in price, or fail to follow your packing and shipping instructions.

*Payment of Bills*

You'll want to make prompt payments to vendors, usually in time to take advantage of their cash discount. Do you realize the high price you pay when you lose cash discounts? For example, the term "3/10 net 30" will "save" you 3 percent of the billed cost if you pay the bill 20 days before it is due. If you can earn $3 on a $100 invoice by a 20 day prepayment, then you can earn $3 × 18, or $54, in a year because there are 18 such 20-day periods in a year. Because the prepayment requires only $97, not $100, your annual saving rate is $54 divided by $97, or 56 percent. Losing such an opportunity as this is an exorbitant price to pay for keeping funds in your business 20 days longer than you would otherwise.

Making funds available for prompt payment is not always easy, but even a high borrowing rate will usually be less than the annual rate of lost discounts.

## Merchandising

Buying for your store requires you to be aware of a number of different things. You need to be aware of changing trends, your changing customers and changing products. To stay abreast of these changes you should:

- read trade journals and newspapers, consumer and business publications

- talk to customers, salespeople, and vendors

- see all manufacturers and their different lines of merchandise

- attend sporting events

In short, as the buyer for your store you should stay alert to new merchandising horizons and new selling opportunities.

**Pricing**

The average for beginning retail markups is 50 percent of retail or 100 percent of wholesale. What this means is if you pay $10 for an item from your wholesale supplier, you'll put a $20 price tag on it.

It's important to remember that this is only an average. Some stores set higher beginning markups, with 55 or 60 percent being fairly common. Some stores use lower beginning markups. If you're carrying product lines which are generally sold at a particular markup by your competitors, you'll need to have about the same markup in order to remain competitive. Your supplier can advise you on standard markups. Some merchandise is preticketed with the retail price or "suggested price." These products are usually brands which have been nationally advertised at a particular price.

To set the prices which will most benefit your store you'll need to customize your pricing based on the following factors:

- The characteristics of your target market, and particularly your customers' willingness to pay a given price for a given item.

- The cost of the product to you.

- Any additional costs associated with the product, such as advertising, overhead, and shipping costs.

- The profit you need to make.

As you figure markups on individual items keep in mind that it is not necessary to make the same profit on every product you carry. What is important is that your overall pricing mix will allow you to make the profit you need. Don't forget that you will be marking some items down later on, and this will lower your overall profit margin.

**Advertising**

Your first step in setting up an advertising program is to map out your objectives. You must pinpoint the customer target you want to reach and plan the most cost-effective method of reaching your target. If your target is middle-income homemakers, find out where they live, which newspapers they read, and which radio stations they listen to.

Most likely, your local newspaper is a member of the American Newspaper Publishers Association and thus has access to its excellent advertising guides. The National Retail Merchants Association has similar guides. Both can show you sound but simple methods for budgeting your advertising over the year. Both stress that good advertising requires you (1) to set sales goals by merchandise classifications, at least 30 days ahead; (2) to budget the amount of advertising you will need to meet these goals; and (3) to decide on the specific items you want to promote and schedule on specific days. Making use of such assistance and the data many manufacturers will gladly provide, you can develop intelligent advertising campaigns and prepare professional-looking advertising at minimum cost.

*Regularity of Advertising*

Advertising regularly was once considered of paramount importance for even the small retailer. It was thought that getting your message across every day or week, even if the ad was tiny, was a wise approach.

Today it's considered more important to have a compelling story to tell, and to tell it dramatically in ample space, than merely to chirp "me too" at regular intervals. You can make a greater impact on your community by mounting a well conceived promotion — requiring full page ads every month or so at important dates in each season — than by making run-of-the-mill little announcements every day or so.

This means, of course, that you should make a continuing search for special promotional goods to supplement your regular stock assortments. If your store is a headquarters for national brands, you should be able to get closeouts and specials from these sources late in each season.

One very successful merchant says he gets ideas for special promotional goods by checking on the special offerings of stores in the large cities. From a trade service and direct contact, he learns of the public's response to these promotions. It is not hard to locate the suppliers of the products, and he has bought and successfully promoted many "hot" items in this way.

*Institutional Advertising*

Part of your advertising budget will go to promote your store's image rather than specific merchandise. You'll want to select certain special qualities to emphasize — for example, broad assortments in certain lines and outstanding personal service. Occasional ads devoted to these institutional purposes don't bring in immediate traffic, but they do build for the future. You can't measure their results quickly, but this is no reason to avoid them.

*Cooperative Advertising*

Many manufacturers of branded products give advertising allowances. There is usually a maximum amount they will allow, and each retailer's portion is related to his purchases. Federal law requires that all such allowances be provided to competing dealers on proportionally equal terms. Unfortunately, many manufacturers find it difficult to maintain this proportionality, and as a result the small store may not always receive its fair share. If you suspect you're not getting the allowances you're supposed to, ask the manufacturer to clarify his policy and make sure you are getting your share.

Even though you insist on advertising money when it is due you from your manufacturers, don't stock a line merely because allowances come with it. As purchasing agent for your customers, your primary consideration is the suitability of the merchandise you buy. Your savings from promotional outlays available on second-rate goods won't offset sluggish sales and the customer ill will you'll reap by stocking goods of questionable quality and style.

Even with top-brand lines, you'll have to be careful in taking advantage of allowance opportunities. You'll help your store's image very little by running an ad just like a number of others around town. Manufacturers are more interested in building demand for their own products than in strengthening your image. Also, even if they provide you with ad mats well conceived in themselves, they will not be carrying out the distinctive image you're trying to establish. Be sure to insist on considerable freedom in layout, copy, and timing of your cooperative ads. Naturally, manufacturers have a right to considerable say in how their funds are spent, but they must also understand that you have your own legitimate interests in making every ad build your store as well as their products.

*Creating the Advertising Campaign*

There are four main steps to follow when creating an advertising campaign:

1. Research — find out everything possible about the products you want to advertise and the people most likely to buy them. Make a checklist of the ways and areas in which you are superior to, equal to, or behind the competition.

2. Strategic planning — determine the results you expect and want, allocate money to the advertising budget, decide on your "creative" approach, and study the available media.

3. Tactical decisions — actual purchasing of media (newspaper space, radio/TV time).

4. Construction of your ad — writing copy, preparing artwork and layout for the finished ad.

*Budgeting and Timing*

You'll need to make the best possible use of your limited advertising budget by planning expenditures effectively. Coordination of your advertising program with your buying schedule is essential — a promotion which is not backed up by merchandise can do more harm than good.

Timing is possibly the most important single consideration in planning effective advertising. Timing involves adjusting your advertising plans to the seasonal patterns of the store, to the store's special days, and to the community's special events. If you are located in a college town you should plan to advertise specials over football weekends and during other student-oriented events of the year. You should also advertise in the school paper and other student publications.

*Media and Copy*

A retailer can choose media from newspaper, radio, television, magazines, direct mail materials, billboards, handbills, goodie bags (a collection of different freebies from a variety of stores put in one bag), and point-of-purchase displays. The target market must be defined before an appropriate combination of media can be chosen. You must ask "Whom do I want as my customers? Who needs my products? Who will buy my products?" It is essential to note that advertising in just one medium may not effectively reach your target market.

It may be helpful to compare your advertising plans with what other sporting goods retailers are doing. According to the NSGA, sporting goods advertising is heavily concentrated in newspapers, where 70 percent of the advertising budget is typically allocated. Of the remaining dollars, 10 percent is allocated to radio, and 5 percent each to direct mail and television. Ten percent of the advertising budget is typically used for miscellaneous purposes and special sales promotions.

You must also determine the type of advertising copy most appropriate to the particular image you are seeking. All advertising copy, however, should observe the basic rules of eye appeal, simplicity, brevity, straightforwardness, and credibility. Use words that are emotion-packed and easy to understand.

## SHOULD YOU OFFER CREDIT?

Providing retail credit requires considerably more cash than is necessary in a cash-and-carry business. The cost of merchandise — not to mention the profit — is not returned to the credit retailer for at least one month and, in some instances it takes one to three years. As an example, under certain conditions it is estimated that a merchant will need $35,000 to $40,000 to carry installment sales credit amounting to $10,000 a month. The additional income produced through a finance charge should eventually warrant the extra cost of offering credit, however, and credit arrangements typically generate additional sales.

Of course, the extension of credit has its disadvantages, especially if the customer fails to repay in full. When collections begin to fall off on accounts receivable, capital reserves must be drawn upon in order to continue in business. Attempts to recover unpaid accounts through professional collectors may help, but as the accounts receivables age, chances for collection rapidly decline.

## EXPANSION

Whenever you attempt to expand a one-person retail operation, you must let go of some day-to-day operations and become a manager. Management is essentially composed of six functions:

- planning
- coordinating
- organizing
- supervising
- staffing
- controlling

Management does *not* include actually doing routine tasks; that is turned over to others. If you've always felt it's easier to do a job yourself than to delegate it to someone else, you may have a difficult time adjusting to the responsibilities of management.

## Personnel Policies

It is difficult to imagine growth in a retail sporting goods business without also thinking of the additional employees the growth will require. Setting and revising personnel policies is an important part of long-range planning. Try to anticipate the situations that can be expected to arise in the business life of every employee. Set up uniform ways of dealing with them rather than expecting to treat each situation as a special case.

Every store, but especially fast growing stores, should have policies governing such matters as wages, promotions, vacations, grievances, fringe benefits, retirement, etc. The degree of detail will increase as your staff is enlarged. Of course, exact policies will differ with the location of your store, the image you are trying to create, and your size and financial stability.

You should set up certain employment and training procedures as well as policies. With them, you have a better chance of getting the work done in an organized and economical way with emphasis on high standards of selection and training.

To the majority of employees, wages are not the chief benefit they derive from a job. What they want most of all is recognition. Many times you can improve morale through salary increases, but often you can stimulate it even more by a word of commendation, an award publicized throughout the community, or an opportunity to qualify for new or more interesting work. Of course, don't forget the other assets that employees seek from any job: reasonable security, a pleasant working environment, and fringe benefits such as health insurance.

Remember, however, that salary is often the first consideration at the time of employment. Thus your wage scales must be competitive with those of other stores in your area. For most positions, your best bet is to offer a straight salary, with review after the first six months of employment and annually thereafter. For sales people you can use the extra stimulus of a small commission on all sales or sales above a quota.

**Physical Expansion**

As your retail operation expands you'll be faced with needing more space or better use of existing space. In making long-range plans you'll be faced with the following options:

- Modernizing existing space, perhaps with some expansion of selling space.

- Opening a branch, or relocating your store in the same metropolitan area.

- Relocating the store itself or establishing a branch in another community.

If you are fortunate enough to locate your original store in an area that will experience steady growth in the type of population you draw your customers from, you may be able to expand simply by modernizing your existing space from time to time. To help you decide about expanding, you'll want to make a careful analysis of the statistical and qualitative data you can get from local real estate boards, chambers of commerce, your bank, and other services. What you'll hope to find is evidence that the group from which you are drawing your existing customers is increasing in numbers and purchasing power, and that new customers can frequently be attracted to your location in considerable numbers. If you can determine these two factors exist, you may decide to stay put and modernize your store to attract the new customer mix.

Alternately, you may decide it's best to seek a new location outside your present city and its suburbs. Perhaps your area is dependent upon a sagging industry; the local political situation may be poor for future prosperity; or perhaps your store has already exploited its specialized local market. Whatever the cause, it may become desirable to select a location elsewhere in making your growth plans.

Here your chief consideration is the growth trend of the customer group or target your type of operation is best fitted to serve. For example, if you have a fine specialty store in a city, you can probably determine the patronage you draw from smaller towns in the area. (Mail orders would be a good indication, and your salespeople could be alerted to identifying out-of-town customers.)

From the information you gather, you will need to judge whether or not your store is known to the discriminating customers living in the locations under consideration. After you have sufficient usable evidence and decide to open a branch, you will want to select the town with the clearest evidence of growth in the type of customers you currently serve.

**Expansion Through Diversification**

Another approach to expanding your sporting goods business is to offer services related to your retail specialty.

Steve Weaver's experience is a case in point. Steve owns a dive shop and has been forced to take this type of diversified approach because his shop is located inland in an area where diving conditions are poor. He opened his shop in spite of this because he felt there were a disproportionate number of active young people with high incomes in the area who could be interested in learning to scuba dive.

Steve's strategy was to provide organized diving tours to the Caribbean and courses in diving as on-going services available through his shop. He sees recruiting new divers, certifying them, and keeping them interested in diving as interrelated parts of his overall business: "There have to be divers to be able to build the rest of your business — to buy equipment, to go on trips, to do whatever. So that is the main thing — you want to keep certifying people, and . . . keep them interested in diving over the long run.

. . . What I mean by that is organizing clubs, offering slide presentations periodically . . . running the trips, sending out a periodical newsletter, advertising — just to keep them interested. And then you try to get them into advanced education, because that will just keep them more interested. Hopefully, once you get them into that, and they see all the possibilities there are in the sport, they'll want to go on [and continue diving] themselves.''

The important point here is that you don't want to define your business too narrowly. If Steve had only opened his retail shop and defined his business strictly as retailing, it's extremely doubtful that it would have been very successful (considering his location). By realizing he was essentially in the business of promoting scuba diving, however, he was able to develop related services which complemented his retail business as well as providing additional income.

# Chapter 5
# Other Opportunities in Sports

Sporting goods retailing, covered in the previous chapter, is an obvious type of sports-related self-employment opportunity. This chapter looks at a number of not-so-obvious opportunities with at least as much potential as retailing and possibly even more potential.

## SPORTS PROMOTION AND EVENTS MANAGEMENT

Sports promoters and events managers are entrepreneurs who organize and stage events. Major sports events are worth a lot of money to their sponsors because, assuming they attract large enough crowds, they are excellent opportunities for advertising and for reaping the benefits of favorable publicity.

Setting yourself up as a sports promoter or events manager requires you to begin thinking of generating income (making sales) in a way that's much different from most other businesses. When spectators gather at the Boston Marathon or the Coors Bicycle Classic, they may not pay a fee to watch but they are the consumers nevertheless, and indirectly, they are the ones who make the event profitable. But from the entrepreneur's point of view, the event's sponsors foot the bill, and this puts the promoter in the position of being the seller and puts the decision-makers within sponsoring corporations in the position of being the direct buyers.

Most people are not aware that when a race is held, a sports exhibition takes place, or a tournament is held at a local club, a sports promoter has probably been at work behind the scenes. Often this is an individual who has simply recognized a need (and an opportunity) and proceeded to organize and promote the event and raise funds from sponsors to pay the tab — including his own fee.

The sponsors of such sporting events are usually large business corporations. And, although many people don't realize it, sponsorship has become such big business that major sporting events are now tailored to fit their sponsors (whereas before sporting events would be planned first with sponsors lined up later).

According to an article in the *Wall Street Journal* on the "Budweiser Cleveland 500" auto race, "without the corporate sponsorship, the race simply wouldn't exist.

". . . The Cleveland 500 didn't just happen to attract sponsors [including Budweiser, Pentax, Minolta, Hertz, and others]. The race's promoters built it around corporate sponsorship from the start. The thousands of dollars that each sponsor pays to have its name associated with the race will combine with ticket sales and cable TV revenues to pay the winning drivers and their crews, along with the race's promoter, Cleveland-based C.K. Newcomb & Associates."

## What Sports Promoters Do

Robert Hackworth is a promoter and events manager whose biggest project has been a runners' expo that involved 48 exhibitors and included seminars, clinics, commercial exhibits, a film festival, fashion show, and exhibits presented by world-class athletes. It coincided with an annual 18,000-person road race in Boulder, Colorado and was, in Robert's words, an effort to expand "the running experience into more than just running the race that morning and make it into more of a festival and a weekend event."

Robert says he "just evolved" into a promoter and, at first, had to convince himself that there was nothing wrong with being a promoter. "A lot of people have a bad connotation about the word 'promoter.' They think of this cigar-smoking guy in the back room setting up fights or something. Maybe I had that impression too, and that's why it took me a while to get there. That's really what I do: I create an idea or event and then I promote it and follow it through from start to finish.''

Mark Buchanan is a sports promoter who, with two others, formed a partnership called Rainbow Sports International. Their first endeavor involves establishing a bicycle team, producing a video project, and managing a small event, but Mark envisions branching out to a variety of other areas. There are too many opportunities available to specialize and therefore become limited to one kind of event, he says. ''If you can deal with one, you can deal with the other. . . . If we're successful in the cycling realm, why not expand and go to the running world, or the golf world, or the tennis world, or motor sports, or anything? What we plan to do as we expand . . . [is to] bring other people in who are specialists [in particular fields].''

Mark sees himself as a middleman. When he finds a sponsor willing to finance a bicycling team, for example, he charges the sponsor a management fee and also collects a ''finder's fee'' from the rider who earns a monthly salary, paid from the funds provided by the sponsor. Rainbow Sports International is also involved in a project that will include production of a television program. The sponsor will pay for the production of the program and will receive commercial time in return. When production is finished, ''we would sell [the program] to either cable or network TV, and of course they would pay us for the finished product also." Such multi-faceted projects involve "an awful lot of money" according to Mark.

Mark Fairbairn organizes racquetball tournaments. He views what he does in the following terms: "Basically I'm just a catalyst that brings together a site for the play and the corporate backing to pull it off in a profitable manner. . . . [I] contact the players that [I] know would be interested in playing, and basically produce and direct the whole thing."

It probably is apparent by now that since only a portion of your income — if any at all — will come from the participants or spectators at your event, your success as a promoter will depend on how well you are able to convince the decision makers in the business world not only that they should sponsor the event but also that you are the person best able to insure that it is a good investment for them. To succeed as a promoter you must learn to effectively communicate with potential sponsors, acquire an understanding of their needs, and explain to them how you can help them meet those needs.

**Why Businesses Sponsor**

Sporting events sponsorship can be an excellent means of advertising. According to the article in the *Wall Street Journal*, "There aren't precise studies showing what sponsorship is worth, but the rule of thumb is that putting $1,000 behind a sports event will generate the same exposure as $10,000 in advertising.'' One company that sponsored a Bermuda-to-New York wind surfer spent $15,000 and figured it was worth $150,000 in publicity, according to the article. And, sponsorship offers the added bonus of providing an opportunity to entertain clients, customers, and employees.

Mark Buchanan says, ''We think it is real visible and real cost effective, and also good [public] relations for the company . . . to be associated with a fitness, health-oriented activity. For x amount of dollars, they can sponsor a cycling team for a summer and get pretty good press and so forth. It depends on how the team does, and that depends, of course, on how much money they want to put up.

''My gosh, you get a picture of a guy coming across the finish line with his hand raised up, and it says 7-Eleven across the jersey. What could be better? No advertisement in a paper is going to help 7-Eleven like that will.''

Chris Reveley, founder of the American Mountain Foundation, says he believes the benefits of sponsorship are ''a good healthy game on both sides of the court because those corporations *have to* give that money away — they'll be taxed into oblivion otherwise.''

But, Robert Hackworth advises, ''you have to be careful about having a product that justifies their sponsorship. . . . You don't ask people to give money just out of their good nature. You ask them to give something because they're going to get something in return for it. Unless you can prove to them that they'll get at least as much as they put into it, then there's no sense in presenting it to them. . . . . There has to be a justification for them to participate and a real value which you can associate with their investment.''

"What it boils down to is, 'will it increase sales?' If it does, then it is worth it; if it doesn't, then it's not worth it,'' he says.

At his running expo, Robert Hackworth made it "worth it" to the commercial exhibitors in this way: he charged each exhibitor $450 for booth space, and he expected 25,000 people to attend. Participation in the expo, then, cost the exhibitors less than two cents per contact with each potential buyer, which is much less than they would expect to pay if they advertised in a running magazine, for example. "It would be much more expensive and there wouldn't be that hands-on and face-to-face type of meeting like there would be at the show,'' he notes. And, he says, the interchange with runners was higher in quality at the show because company representatives could make comparisons with their competition's products in ways that are not acceptable in print or electronic media advertising.

Of what benefit is an events manager to a club hosting a tournament? A manager who takes care of organizing the tournament from start to finish frees up the club's staff to maintain and promote the club. Events manager Mike Keel explains that because he organizes and conducts the tournament, the club's employees are better able to take advantage of the opportunity to promote the club and its classes and lessons. "When they are doing the tournament, they don't have any time to give that a thought," Mike says.

## Why Companies Depend on Independent Promoters

You might wonder why companies like Anheuser-Busch and Nike (or your local club, for that matter) don't just employ events managers and sports promoters since these activities are a regular part of their budgets. Essentially it's not cost effective to do so because the activity is too specialized. And remember, Budweiser may have shelled out big bucks to sponsor the Cleveland 500, but it was only one of several sponsors involved in the road race. Events like that are organized much more efficiently if one manager, or management organization, handles it all.

It's been Mark Buchanan's experience that sponsors don't want responsibility for the overall event, either. "It's something they don't want to do, and it's something they don't have the knowledge about," he says. "Somebody has to pull it together. A lot of the events don't go off well because sixteen different companies or sponsors are trying to work together, and that's never going to work. What we would hope to do is be the central core, pull everything together, please everybody, be a liaison between all the groups, and cater to their needs."

**The Cost of Publicity**

What a company can expect to get out of the event depends, of course, on how much they contribute. But some of the benefits they receive from sponsorship might include:

- use of their name and/or logo on such items as entry forms, signs, scoreboards, etc.
- banners hanging in conspicuous places with the company name
- an advertisement in the event's program
- use of the company's product in the event (such as a drink at the aid stations in a race, for example)
- media exposure
- face-to-face contact with potential buyers
- tax benefits

A number of factors affect how much publicity a company will receive for its sponsorship. If a company wants to sponsor a racing team, for example, it will receive more exposure if it funnels enough money into the team to enable the manager to hire winning racers and provide other resources necessary to make the team competitive. Sponsorships can involve a few hundred dollars, several thousand dollars, or more. Having an event or a widely known team named after one's company might cost thousands, while a name on the entry forms might cost one of the many co-sponsors $50 to $500.

**Repeat Performances**

Promoters of sports events make most of their profit on events which are repeated on a regular basis. From a promoter's point of view, events held on an annual (or some other regular) basis require much less time, effort, and money after the first year than do one-time events. Robert Hackworth found this to be true for him when he organized the running expo. "To get a new event started, it takes so much ground work and you have to make so many new contacts [the first year] it really is a full-time job." The second and subsequent years are relatively simple, however, and "if it is a good show, . . . your exhibitors will be back, and then you've got a formula of how you're going to do it the second year. . . . You just fill in the blank spaces," Robert says.

What's more, you're likely to make more money on the second or subsequent events than you make on the first. Clearly sports promotion and events management should be considered a long-term effort.

Not all sports events are large scale productions requiring multiple sponsors, of course. The initial investment for organizing a running race, for example, may be no more than a few hundred dollars. For this reason, races can be an easy way to enter the sports promotion/events management business. However, as Colin Lippencott, a budding race organizer, says, "It's easy in, easy out. Therefore, there is a very high potential of low returns."

Obviously, some of your expenses can be offset

if you sponsor a participatory event and charge an entrance fee. Why do people pay to participate in an event? Of course part of the reason is simply that such events are fun, but Colin offers another reason. Everyone "likes to be recognized for their achievements," he says. "They want some attention. They want people to notice them. . . . People will pay for recognition."

## CONSULTING AND RECREATION BROKERING

As we've seen with sports promotion, companies often get involved in activities that are outside their areas of expertise, and it is not economically feasible for them to employ a staff a full-time specialists in all fields. Instead, they do business with consultants when the need arises — and in rapidly growing fields like the sports industry that happens frequently. A manufacturer of running shoes may sponsor races, promote running, sponsor athletes, and generally ally itself with the fitness field, and sports consultant Rich Castro is an example of the kind of person such a company will turn to for specialized help.

Rich's services are valuable because, as he says, "they can find a number of people who know different areas [of the running business], but I know the athletes, I know the race directors, I put the major road racing lists together. . . . I'm out in the field, I work with elite athletes, I experiment with new forms of training, I do lectures, and I'm also familiar with the facets of road racing such as the track trusts. . . . In other words, I have the whole picture, and they . . . [only] have slices of it.''

Consulting is different from events management and sports promotion in that it involves a more traditional business arrangement. That is, a business needs a service and calls in a specialist to provide it.

Paul Betters is also a sports consultant, but he concentrates on market research. A client of Paul's may be a manufacturer who has a problem with one of his products. The product may not be selling as well as it should because of the way it is perceived in the marketplace, for example. Paul provides the information needed for the company to make sound decisions about "repositioning" the product. Very few companies are able to keep up with all the developments in their field, making Paul's help extremely valuable.

**Employee Programs**

Miriam Gingras has assembled a group of eight individuals, including a physician, an exercise physiologist, a psychologist, a physical therapist, a registered dietitian, a sports psychologist, and an occupational health nurse, to consult with corporations on employee fitness. In dealing with corporate executives, Miriam emphasizes that health training and prevention of illness and injury is less expensive than treatment after the fact and that physical fitness contributes to increased productivity.

Miriam offers three broad types of services: consulting (which includes worksite health assessment, analysis of biomechanical risk factors in the workplace, program planning, and evaluation of the company's fitness program), seminars (which include workshops on diet, stress management, prevention of heart and back problems, hypertension, and motivation), and ongoing programs (including testing, classes in CPR, first aid and weight control, and coaching for corporate teams). Her clients pay $75 an hour for consulting or $700 for an all-day seminar. Miriam's business retains 55 percent of the fee, and the consultants in her group receive the remaining 45 percent.

Miriam reports that her seminars are in greatest demand. This came as a surprise to her because she thought her fitness classes would be the biggest seller. She attributes this to the failure of corporate executives to fully commit themselves to fitness programs and to the fact that only a small percentage of the people in her market actually participate in fitness activities. Also, this is a relatively new field, and there are only limited data on the benefits of fitness programs to the sponsoring company. Short-term assessments of similar programs at New York Telephone Company, NASA, and General Motors have been very favorable, however. Their endorsements give the field some momentum, and logic alone prompts some companies to sample programs like Miriam's.

### Recreation Brokering

Don Parkin has also seized an opportunity in the corporate world and found a unique niche for himself. He realized that people attending conventions and meetings away from home often seek recreation but are too unfamiliar with the area to know what is available. And, he observed, recreation businesses are often underexposed in the market at large. So the concept of a recreation brokerage — which would match recreation providers with their customers — naturally occured to Don.

Organizations customarily contract with "meeting planners" to coordinate conventions and conferences. These specialists take care of all the details of a convention, freeing the executives within the organization from this burden. If the people attending the conference would like a particular type of recreation, that message is relayed to the meeting planner, who then gets in touch with a recreation broker such as Don. He arranges the activity with one of the recreation businesses associated with him. Don does not charge the convention planner or company sponsoring the convention; instead, he takes a 10 percent commission of whatever the recreation business is paid.

Don selects the businesses he sends customers to after a series of interviews, an on-site inspection, and completion of a questionnaire.

Although association with a broker increases a recreation business's access to customers, it doesn't guarantee an increase in sales. Don may not receive many requests for rock climbing, for example, so he can't predict how much business he will be able to send a climbing outfit in any given time. But a recreation broker is almost always lining up business for someone.

**Specialized Recreation Brokering**

Dick Gould is a tennis broker. He has positioned himself between city recreation departments, which regularly offer tennis classes, and tennis instructors. He locates tennis teachers (which isn't difficult since he is head tennis coach at Stanford University), trains them, puts together a quarterly schedule of offerings, and presents the schedule to recreation departments of the cities he serves.

The departments are receptive because they are assured of qualified teachers year after year and of a coherent and continuous offering of classes. Dick's services are helpful to the instructors because he has contracts in twenty cities. Dick charges each city a fee for his services and pays the instructors from the proceeds.

**Finding Your Own Niche**

The key to succeeding in your own consulting or recreation brokering business is to develop your own unique service approach to your particular area of expertise. As Rich Castro says, "you have to tell . . .

[your clients] what needs to be created. . . . That's what a person needs to do — literally create your own niche . . . and you also have to be unafraid of setting some very high standards for yourself."

One way Rich has promoted his services was to write letters to business executives spelling out what he wanted to do for them, identifying their needs, and explaining how he could help them meet those needs. "I told them what areas I had been covering. . . . It worked tremendously. I just went right to the top. I didn't . . . [bother] with anybody else down below," Rich says.

## SPORTSWRITING

An interesting thing has happened to sportswriting in the last few years. As sports have evolved into a national pastime (some would say obsession), some sportswriters have risen to a celebrity status — and pay scale — approaching that of the superstar athletes they report on. And, like the media celebrities they cover, some sportswriters have become essentially free agents, providing their services to the highest bidder.

Consider the following:

- To hire sportswriter Skip Bayless away from the *Dallas Morning News*, the *Dallas Times Herald* reportedly offered a five-year contract worth about $500,000. Included in the offer was a clause prohibiting Mr. Bayless's dismissal, as well as an understanding that his columns would be subjected to little or no editing.

* Woodrow "Woody" Paige Jr. now makes $75,000 a year covering sports for *The Denver Post* after being hired away from the *Rocky Mountain News*, according to an article in the *Wall Street Journal*. This does not include the income from his radio and television shows, however.

* Dick Young switched from the *New York Daily News* to the *New York Post* for an undisclosed sum. It must have been substantial, however, because the *Daily News* filed a $750,000 lawsuit against him, charging that he broke his $100,000 contract in making the move.

These are clearly exceptional cases but they do indicate the potential that exists if you have an engaging writing style and a strong interest in sports.

It's not necessary to get a degree in journalism and start out as a cub reporter in order to write about sports, of course. Most established writers recommend starting on a part-time basis, submitting articles to newspapers and magazines while keeping your current job. This allows you to hone your writing skills and develop a feel for the sportswriting market without risk.

## The Sports Magazine Market

There have been some major changes in magazines since 17-year-old Bob Anderson hand-folded and hand-stapled the first issue of a magazine he put together for runners. That magazine, which he started with the grand sum of $100, is today known as *Runner's World*.

In many ways the rags-to-riches experience of *Runner's World* reflects the fundamental changes occuring in the magazine industry in the last two decades. General interest mass market magazines have faltered, faced with declining circulations and declining advertising revenues. An incredible array of specialty magazines — including *Runner's World* — have sprung up to replace them as consumers have come to demand more highly specialized information.

The result of these changes is a larger market for freelance articles than there has ever been before. There are currently more than 100 publications devoted specifically to sports, for example, with another 60 or so devoted to fishing, hunting, and camping. More publishers than ever are searching for fresh ideas, new talent, and good copy.

There's also another way that specialization in the magazine market helps freelancers. By specializing you can write more efficiently because your research is more focused. As you become familiar with researching your field, you save time because you're not continually trying to identify unfamiliar information sources.

**Researching the Market**

Please don't get the idea that making a comfortable living writing freelance sports articles is easy, however. In spite of the growth of specialty magazines in general, and sports magazines in particular, freelance writing remains a demanding and highly competitive occupation.

The key to succeeding in this field is to thoroughly research the publications which are most likely to carry your type of articles. Two resources are especially helpful for this, and the chances are good that your local library has both. *Writer's Market* and *Literary Market Place* give the requirements for articles in literally thousands of publications. This is where you want to start your search, but it is only the beginning. Some publications will provide writer's guidelines to anyone interested in writing for them, and you should definitely request these and study them carefully.

Most importantly, though, you need to read and study the specific publications you're interested in writing for. You need to fully understand the editorial slant, style, and reader characteristics of a publication before even sending a query letter to the editor.

The best way to analyze a magazine in this way is to get a number of back issues together and take notes as you go through them. First look at the article titles. Try to see what the common denominators are and what categories the articles logically fall into. Then look over each issue individually, making notes as you go and paying attention not only to the articles but also to editorials, columns, ads, and Letters to the Editor. As you familiarize yourself with a given publication you'll learn what is required to tailor your articles to that particular market. Try to form a mental image of the individuals who regularly read the magazine, and offer information which will appeal to and interest those individuals. Remember that magazines feature articles that satisfy their readers and cater directly to the needs of their readers, and you're wasting your time sending them anything that doesn't fit these criteria.

**Dealing with Publishers**

As you look through *Writer's Market, Literary Market Place*, and the guidelines individual publications send you, you'll probably come across a number of terms which may be unfamiliar to you. If you deal with publishers you'll need to understand their editorial requirements, which often include the following terms:

- *Simultaneous, photocopied, and previously published submissions OK.* This means that the editor will not care if you send the same article (or a rewrite) to other noncompetitive publications at the same time you send it to him. It is not necessary to send an original manuscript, and it doesn't matter if the article has previously been published — as long as the other publication is not a direct competitor.

- *POP.* This stands for "pays on publication." It is always preferable to be paid on acceptance rather than on publication.

- *Phone queries OK.* Most editors prefer to be queried in writing, and unless you see this notation you should assume that the editor doesn't want to be bothered by phone calls. If you have a hot story that is extremely timely and won't wait for the mail, you should probably make an exception.

- *No byline.* Some publications buy articles from freelancers but have a policy against naming the authors of such material. This is unfortunate for you, since building a reputation as a freelancer largely depends on having your byline seen prominently and frequently.

- *Kill fee.* Once you become established, editors will assign stories to you. A kill fee is money to be paid for your work on the story if the magazine decides *not* to publish the assigned article. This may be a set amount or it may be negotiable.

- *Captions required.* If you provide photos with your article be sure to include a short explanation, including the identities of anyone pictured in the photo.

- *Model release.* Magazines often require subjects pictured in photos to sign a liability release form to protect against libel, slander, invasion of privacy, etc.

**Article Ideas**

How can you consistently come up with interesting, salable ideas for magazines? First of all, it's important to realize that any article idea actually consists of both a subject and an angle. The angle is the slant you use to make the subject interesting to a particular group of people.

One way to produce ideas is to use a brainstorming technique. Simply set aside fifteen or twenty minutes and quickly jot down or type as many article ideas as you can come up with, paying no attention whatsoever (at the moment) to whether the ideas are good, bad, or indifferent. Many people find that by deliberately suspending critical judgment in this way they can regularly come up with creative ideas.

It can also be helpful to make a long list of articles which personally spark your interest from a number of different magazines. Try to pinpoint exactly what makes the articles appeal to you, and look for gaps in subject coverage and new angles on the same subjects. You may find that going through this process first, prior to deliberately suspending judgment using the brainstorming technique, will produce the best results.

Attending sporting events, talking with all different types of sports enthusiasts, going to sporting goods business conventions — any type of activity related to your interest in sports can stimulate new article ideas. You'll need to get in the habit of always carrying a pad and pen so you can jot down words, phrases and ideas as they occur to you. As you gain experience, you'll probably find yourself developing a keen sense of observation, and eventually new article ideas will occur to you with very little effort.

**Tips for Successful Freelancing**

Establishing yourself as a freelance sports writer will take time and a great deal of practice. By observing the following guidelines you may be able to speed up the process somewhat:

- Write about what you know and constantly study your chosen area of interest. Articles by recognized experts in a particular field are always in demand, so work on becoming a recognized expert.

- Query editors before sending your manuscript. Otherwise it will probably end up in the slush pile with countless others.

- Write with directness and simplicity. Strive to put life into your narrative by using anecdotes and dialogue or pertinent quotes.

- Always send a neat, typewritten manuscript and include a stamped, self-addressed envelope if you want the manuscript back.

- Remember that the more useful information you can give the reader the more valuable your article will be. A guide listing useful addresses, tips, references or other items, often included as a separate box or added at the end of an article, is an added touch that readers — and editors — often appreciate.

- Realize that magazines want articles handled their own way. Tailor your article to the specific focus of a given publication.

- Be persistent and constantly keep ideas before an editor. As soon as one article is accepted, immediately try to get a new project approved by the same editor. By always keeping your name before an editor you'll establish yourself, and that means you'll start receiving assignments based on the editor's own article ideas.

Finally, always try to sell the same basic article as many times as you possibly can. Simply try to figure out all the possible markets for a given idea. Regularly go back through your sold articles to find ways that you can resell the same material, realizing that small changes may make a manuscript acceptable to other markets. Be careful, however, to clearly mark your manuscript "second rights" or "simultaneous submission" when appropriate.

**Spinoffs from Freelance Writing**

Some freelance sports writers find that spinoff activities, such as photography and lecturing, can nicely complement their writing and open up entirely new opportunities.

Glenn Randall is a freelance writer specializing in the outdoors, travel, wildlife, climbing, and skiing. He has been freelancing for five years now, and it's not unusual for him to spend seventy to ninety hours a week writing. He often includes photos with his articles, and somehow he is finding the time to organize his 7,000 slides so he can establish his photography as a business in its own right. Once he has his stock photos organized into categories he intends to computerize his list and mail it to 100 or so potential customers every three months or so. Since he uses his photography in his writing anyway, he has little risk in trying to establish this type of sideline.

John Harlin is also a freelance writer. His most recent undertaking is a six-volume climbing guide covering all of North America — a project which requires him to spend at least half of his time on the road visiting climbing areas.

John uses photographs in another kind of spin-off which complements his writing — lecturing. He sends out promotional packages describing his lectures on mountaineering and also spends considerable time on the phone promoting his lectures. He has chosen this route instead of going through a lecture agency because he feels that it is more cost effective for the market he is aiming for. This market includes climbing equipment stores, Sierra Club banquets, university outdoor clubs and alumni associations. He makes about $275 per lecture but expects this fee to go upwards to $500 after his six-volume climbing guide is completed and results in new speaking engagements.

## CAPITALIZING ON YOUR IDEAS

Sometimes the right idea at the right time can lead to almost overnight success in manufacturing sports products. The following ideas clearly fall into this category:

- When Eddie Bauer got a case of hypothermia while out in the woods one weekend in 1934 he started thinking about using goose down to provide insulation in clothing. Soon thereafter he began selling a down jacket called the Skyliner. Because he patented the idea he was the only manufacturer allowed to make and sell down clothing for seventeen years. The rest, as they say, is history.

- Sierra Designs founder George Marks got the idea for a new line of tents while looking at photographs of 13th and 14th Century architecture with gothic arches and vaulted domes. The company's Octadome tents are actually copies of St. Peter's Cathedral, and the Aireflex tent is a variation based on vaulted arches.

- At a Shakespeare festival in Vermont two women joggers struck up a conversation about their mutual inability to buy any type of bra that would provide the support needed for jogging. Hinda Schreiber, then an assistant professor at the University of South Carolina, and Lisa Lindahl, a student in the University of Vermont's masters degree program in administration and planning, decided to do something about the situation. They found the solution to their problem not in other bras but in jock straps — by cutting two in half and sowing them together they found they could make a comfortable running bra. When their "jogbra" hit the market it was almost immediately successful.

- Arthur A. Jones got his idea at a time when he was almost totally broke. He borrowed enough cash from his sister to weld together an exercise machine using a new type of cam — resembling the shell of a nautilus mollusk — to vary the resistance provided by a stack of weights. Within a few years his Nautilus machine was bringing in about $300 million a year in sales.

Ideas can be totally innovative or only a slight variation on an existing product. They can also be a different method of packaging, producing, or presenting a product to consumers. Regardless of how much originality is involved in the idea, you should not spend a great deal of money and time on its development until you've first analyzed the idea's marketability.

This point is crucial but it is all too often overlooked. Many ideas appear worthwhile from a theoretical standpoint but relatively few are practical and applicable enough to result in a product with a long and profitable life. Inventors and entrepreneurs often make the mistake of investing in equipment, personnel, and product development before analyzing the marketability of the product.

**Conducting a Feasibility Study**

A feasibility study can help you evaluate what commercial applications, if any, a product based on your idea would have. You need to know what consumers need, how much they are willing to pay, and what competing products are currently available at what prices. If you can also determine the sales volumes of competing products, so much the better.

Conducting a feasibility study requires that you be as objective as possible about your product's chances in the marketplace. It's all too tempting to allow subjective involvement to distort the facts, and decisions based on hunches can be extremely costly.

The factors any feasibility study should examine include:

- the price range acceptable to the market

- anticipated sales volume

- anticipated profit margin

- fixed and variable costs

- distribution plans

This last item, distribution planning, is often overlooked in deciding on the feasibility of a given product idea. There is a tendency to focus strictly on the potential profit of a product without considering the distribution channels which may or may not exist to get the product to market. This is unfortunate because without a well thought out distribution system to effectively deliver the product to retailers (or other markets), even the best of products can fail. Sometimes the best solution is to form a joint venture with another company that already has appropriate distribution channels and market penetration.

## Break-Even Analysis

Your feasiblity study should include a break even analysis which shows you about how much you must sell under given conditions in order to just cover your costs with no profit and no loss. This allows you to see at what approximate level of sales a new product will pay for itself and begin to bring in a profit.

Profit depends on sales volume, selling price, and costs. To figure your break-even point, you first separate your fixed costs, such as rent, from your variable costs per unit, such as materials.

The formula for figuring break-even is:

$$\frac{\text{break-even}}{\text{volume}} = \frac{\text{total fixed costs}}{\text{selling price} - \text{variable cost per unit}}$$

## Your Business Plan

Once you have completed your feasibility study and you're convinced that you should go ahead and develop your product, the next step is to work up a business plan. A business plan is basically a roadmap which lays down the goals of your venture and the methods by which these goals will be met.

There are a number of books which can guide you, step by step, through the process of developing your business plan (see appendix). Remember that the best business plans are simple and concise.

## Prototypes

Once you've finished your business plan, you'll be ready to construct a prototype model of your product. Your prototype should be as similar to the real thing as possible because it will be placed in targeted markets to test its acceptance. It will also provide information for making final refinements.

At this stage you will want to devote considerable attention to the packaging of your product. The size, shape, and color of your packaging, and the readability and believability of your label are absolutely critical. In some market situations, consumers are more influenced by the package than by its contents.

## Protecting Your Idea

Most people are careful not to discuss their invention ideas because they fear having their ideas stolen. That could happen, of course, but that is only one of the reasons for keeping your idea to yourself. The other reason is that once you discuss your invention in public you only have twelve months to file for a patent. After twelve months, an automatic statutory bar goes into effect which prevents you from then obtaining a patent.

### *Obtaining a Patent*

You should understand that only products can

be patented (not ideas or services). How difficult submitting your patent application is will greatly depend on the amount of research involved and the degree of complexity of your product. In any case, you will need the professional help of a patent attorney.

The number of patent applications submitted grows each year, and a backlog of some 200,000 pending applications has created an average waiting period of 25½ months.

That's not the only bad news, though. It costs $150 to file your application, and the issuance fee is another $250. Under a patent your invention will be protected for seventeen years, *if* you pay maintenance fees during this period. Maintenance fees currently amount to $200 after three and a half years, $400 after seven and a half years, and $600 after eleven and a half years. The patent will lapse and become available for public development unless the fees are paid at the specified times.

*Your Notebook*

Possibly the next best protection to a patent is your inventor's notebook. You should always write down your notes, calculations, and the complete development history of your ideas in a bound, dated, and witnessed notebook.

Each entry in your notebook should have the date of the entry in the margin. There may be several entries on any given page, so you need to leave space at the bottom of each page for your signature and the date as well. Periodically you should have your notebook witnessed by someone you trust. Your witness (who should not be a member of your family) should sign each page after the notation "read and understood by me" along with the date. What you are doing, of course, is providing documentary evidence of when you came up with the idea. If someone else comes up with the same idea after you do but before you have applied for a patent, your notebook may be the only protection you have.

*Trademarks*

Trademarks are basically your company's name and the logo you use in marketing your products or services. Trademarks are similar to patents in that they reserve these identifications to your exclusive use. Since a great deal of money may be involved in promoting your products it's important that you complete the trademark registration process at the earliest possible date.

You should register your trademark with the Secretary of State in all of the states where you plan to do business. If you conduct business across state lines you should also register your trademark with the Commissioner of Patents and Trademarks in Washington D.C. Although trademark registration is a relatively simple process, you should seek legal advice about this as well as patents.

# MANUFACTURING

Many people associate manufacturing with assembly lines, steel mills, and smoke stacks, but manufacturing is not always such a capital-intensive, large-scale operation. Some manufacturing firms are small, family-run businesses, and some companies which start with such humble beginnings rapidly grow into multi-million dollar operations.

## Manufacturing on a Shoestring

Eric Bader owns a whitewater equipment shop, but because he produces paddle jackets, spray skirts, throw bags and related products, he is also a manufacturer. "I was forced into the manufacturing," he says, "because I couldn't afford to buy the gear wholesale." He set up a sewing machine, cutting table, and fabric rack in his store and, during the winter when business was slack, began producing his own products to sell. Since he is able to do the labor himself, his only costs for some of his software goods is for materials, and he is able to sell his products for enough to provide a profit in addition to a reasonable rate for his labor. This has been important for Eric because at any one time he has about $20,000 in inventory (at wholesale cost).

In whitewater outfitting, the markup is typically 40 percent over wholesale, whereas in most businesses the markup is 100 percent. Jewelry, Eric mentions with visible envy, is sometimes marked up four or five times: "I wish I could do that, but unfortunately the market won't withstand it. . . . But in manufacturing . . . I get a proper profit margin. I don't think I'd stay in business without the manufacturing."

## The Potential in Starting Small

One night in 1971 Ron and Lenora Gilchrist were sitting around the dining table when they decided they could make swimming goggles that were superior to those currently on the market. Both Ron and Lenora had been competitive swimmers, and they felt that more comfortable goggles would find a ready market.

They had enough confidence in their idea to risk $15,000 of their savings to go into business. Ron took a prototype of their new goggles on the road and met with high school and college swim coaches. The response was enthusiastic and by getting 50 percent cash advances on the resulting orders the Gilchrists were able to begin production.

According to an article in *In Business* magazine, the Gilchrists first sold "private label" goggles. In other words, initial sales went to distributors with established name brands, and it was four years before the Gilchrists took out a $150,000 bank loan and began distributing under their own "Leader Sports" brand.

Now the Gilchrists sell their products through 89 manufacturers' representatives in a variety of sporting goods fields. The number of retail accounts is growing at a rate of 80 a month, and licensed distributors buy their goggles outright for sale to foreign markets.

In addition to swimming goggles, the Gilchrists now manufacture products for a wide variety of sports, including motorcycling, racquetball, skiing, bobsledding, fishing, and hunting. They are currently producing more than a million swimcaps a year, and they produce training films for swimming and diving schools and clubs through their Aqua Forums subsidiary.

In 1982 worldwide sales were more than $6 million.

## THE ULTIMATE JOB

No discussion of the many opportunities in sports would be complete without at least touching on opportunities for self-employment as a performing athlete. While it's true that this is an opportunity which is open to relatively few people, untold numbers of sports buffs dream of nothing else.

For Ellen Hart, the dream became reality. Although she is now the fifth ranked women's road racer, she didn't really plan on becoming a performing athlete: "I kind of just stumbled into this business . . . totally by accident." When she won her first prize money in the 1981 Cascade Runoff in Oregon, it came as a complete surprise to her. After six miles of a 6.2 mile race, Ellen found herself in a sprinting duel for second place. She hadn't even looked at the prize schedule before the race, but when it was over she had won five thousand dollars. Six days later she won another five thousand dollars at the Pepsi Challenge National Championships.

The ten thousand dollars Ellen won in six days made a big impression on her because, as she says, "the previous year I had worked my fingers to the bone" as a teacher, dorm parent, adviser, and coach, and only made $8,000 for the entire year.

Now Ellen is making a career of her running. Her training regimen usually takes five to six hours a day, and involves running, swimming, biking, and weight lifting. In addition, she may have some paperwork connected with her sponsorships, clinics, appearances, lectures, travel, and article writing. It all adds up to a time-consuming job: "there just seem to be all sorts of things connected to my running that end up filling up a whole day. . . . It seems like pretty much the whole day revolves around one aspect or another.

Time consuming or not, if you've got what it takes to successfully compete in a sport, there are opportunities for making endorsements, consultants' fees, and sponsorship money in addition to prize money. It could just be the ultimate job. As Ellen puts it "It's fun to be able to make a living doing what I really enjoy doing. . . . I always wanted to keep playing sports as long as I could . . . but I never thought it would be a career. I don't often tell race promoters this, but I'd be doing most of the things I do now for free, anyway, so to be getting paid on top of it is a big bonus."

## IN CONCLUSION

This chapter has looked at a variety of sports-related self-employment opportunities but no attempt has been made to be comprehensive. The important point to be made is that all sorts of opportunities are opening up in sports as Americans become more recreation- and fitness-minded.

As Chris Reveley, founder of the American Mountain Foundation says, we are at "the dawn of a new era," and there are countless niches for creative entrepreneurs just waiting to be identified and developed. Chris is enthusiastic about his work as a fund raiser and promoter and says, "I think it's great, a way to make a living doing what you want to do, which is really what it is all about."

# APPENDIX
## Sources
## of Additional Information

### RECOMMENDED BOOKS

*Note: Many of these books are available by mail from the New Careers Center, which also has tapes and other materials on self-employment. For the most recent catalog, send your name and address to: New Careers Center, P.O. Box 1758, Denison, Texas 75020.*

**Accounting**

*Efficient Accounting and Record Keeping* by Dennis Doyle. Wiley Press ($6.95)

**Advertising**

*How to Advertise: A Handbook for the Small Business* by Sandra Linville Dean. Enterprise Publishing, 1983 ($9.95)

**Consulting**

*How to Succeed as an Independent Consultant* by Herman Holtz. John Wiley & Sons, 1983 ($19.95)

**Financing Your Business**

*How to Finance Your Small Business With Government Money: SBA Loans* by Rick Stephan Hayes and John Cotton Howell. John Wiley & Sons, 1980 ($14.95)

*Financing Your Small Business* by Egon Loffel. Wiley Press ($4.95)

**Legal**

*Legal Master Guide for Small Business* by Fred Steingold. Prentice-Hall, 1983 ($21.95)

**Office**

*How to Set Up a Business Office: The Complete Guide to Locating, Outfitting and Staffing.* Enterprise Publishing ($14.95)

*Working from Home* by Paul and Sarah Edwards. Jeremy P. Tarcher, Inc., 1984 ($9.95)

**Public Relations**

*How to Get Free Press: A Do-It-Yourself Guide to*

*Promote Your Interests, Organization or Business.* Harbor Publishing, 1981 ($12.95)

**Retailing**

*Open and Operate Your Own Small Store.* Prentice-Hall, 1982 ($15.95)

*Opening Your Own Retail Store* by Lyn Taetzsch. Contemporary Books, 1977 ($8.95)

*Practical Marketing for Your Small Retail Business* by William H. Brannen. Prentice-Hall, 1984 ($7.95)

**Travel Business**

*How to Open and Run a Money-Making Travel Agency* by Pamela Fremont. Wiley Press, 1983 ($8.95)

**General**

*402 Things You Should Know Before Starting Your Own Business* by Joseph R. Mancuso and Phillip J. Fox. Prentice-Hall, ($6.95)

*How to Test Your Million Dollar Idea: A Unique Manual for Would-Be Entrepreneurs.* Bobbs-Merrill Co., 1982 ($13.95)

*In Business for Yourself* by Jerome Goldstein.

Charles Scribner's Sons, 1982 ($12.95). Highly recommended.

*The Small Business Survival Guide* by Joseph Mancuso. Prentice-Hall ($10.95)

*Small-Time Operator: How to Start Your Own Small Business, Keep Your Books, Pay Your Taxes, and Stay Out of Trouble!* by Bernard Kamoroff, C.P.A. Bell Springs Publishing. Updated yearly. Highly recommended.

## TRADE PERIODICALS

*Boating Business*
S/S Publications Ltd.,
Box 673,
Parry Sound
Ontario, Canada

*Boating Industry Magazine*
Whitney Commercial Corporation,
850 Third Ave.
New York, NY 10022

*Bicycle Dealer Showcase*
Hester Communications, Inc.
Box 19531
Irvine, CA 92713

*Bicycle Product News*
Freed-Crown Publishing Co.
6931 Van Nuys Blvd.,
Box 2338
Van Nuys, CA 91405

*Camping Industry*
Fishing Tackle Trade News, Inc.
Box 365
Wilmette, IL 60091

*Camping Products Merchandising*
Hanley Publishing Co.,
3412 Main St.,
Skokie, IL 60076

*International Adventure Travel Guide*
American Adventure Association
444 N.E. Ravenna Blvd.
Seattle, OR 98115

*Outdoor Retailer*
Pacifica Publishing Corp.
Box 348
S. Laguna, CA 92677

*Pro-Sports*
Reese Publishing Co., Inc.
235 Park Ave. South,
New York, NY 10003

*Racquetball Industry*
Industry Publishers
1545 N.E. 123rd St., North
Miami, FL 33161

*River Runner Magazine*
Juniper Publications, Inc.
Powell Butte, OR 97753

*Ski Business*
Nick Hock Associates, Inc.
975 Post Road
Darien, CT 06820

*Ski Industry Letter*
Washington Business Information, Inc.
235 National Press Building
Washington, D.C. 20045

*Skiing Trade News*
(*Wintersport Magazine*)
Ziff-Davis Publishing Co.
1 Park Ave.
New York, NY 10006

*Sports Business*
Princeton Archives
1101-D State Rd.,
Princeton, NJ 08540

*Travel Agent*
American Traveler, Inc.
2 W. 46th St.,
New York, NY 10036

*Travel Agents Marketplace*
Gralla Publications
1515 Broadway
New York, NY 10036

*Travel Trade*
Travel Trade Publications, Inc.
6 East 46th St.,
New York, NY 10017

## TRADE ASSOCIATIONS

American Association for Leisure and Recreation
1900 Association Drive.
Reston, VA  22091

American Society of Travel Agents
4400 MacArthur Blvd., N.W.
Washington, D.C. 20007

Association of Physical Fitness Centers
5272 River Road
Suite 500
Washington, D.C. 20016

Association of Racquetsports Manufacturers and Suppliers
8600 W. Bryn Mawr Ave.
Suite 720-S
Chicago, IL 60631

International Association of Tour Managers
100 Bank St.,
Suite 3J
New York, NY 10014

International Racquet Sports Association
Ten Concord Ave.
Cambridge, MA 02138

National Association of Sporting Goods Wholesalers
Box 11344
Chicago, IL 60611

National Bicycle Dealers Association
c/o Bostrom Management Corporation
Tribune Tower,
Suite 1717
435 N. Michigan Ave.
Chicago, IL 60611

National Fitness Association
Box 1754
Huntington Beach, CA 92647

National Ski Touring Operators' Association
Box 557
22 High St.
Brattleboro, VT 05301

National Sporting Goods Association
Lake Center Plaza Building
1699 Wall St.
Mt. Prospect, IL 60056

Ski Retailers Council
600 Madison Ave.
New York, NY 10022

Sporting Goods Agents Association
Box 998
Norton Grove, IL 60053

Sporting Goods Manufacturers Association
200 Castlewood Drive
North Palm Beach, FL 33408

Travel Industry Association of America
1899 L St.
Suite 600
Washington, D.C. 20036

U.S. Association of Independent Gymnastic Clubs
235 Pinehurst Road
Wilmington, DE 19803